THE SEARCH FOR A
NEW PSYCHIATRY

THE SEARCH FOR A NEW PSYCHIATRY

On Becoming a Psychiatrist, Clinical Neuroscientist and Other Fragments of Memory

A. George Awad

THE SEARCH FOR A NEW PSYCHIATRY
ON BECOMING A PSYCHIATRIST, CLINICAL
NEUROSCIENTIST AND OTHER FRAGMENTS OF MEMORY

iUniverse books may be ordered through booksellers or by contacting:

iUniverse
1663 Liberty Drive
Bloomington, IN 47403
www.iuniverse.com
844-349-9409

ISBN: 978-1-6632-2622-8 (sc)
ISBN: 978-1-6632-2623-5 (hc)
ISBN: 978-1-6632-2621-1 (e)

Library of Congress Control Number: 2021914820

Print information available on the last page.

iUniverse rev. date: 07/21/2021

CONTENTS

Part VIII: Psychiatric Outcomes

Part IX: Current Psychiatric Practices

DEDICATION

To my wife, Lara, and our son, Michel (Michael)

I have enjoyed Lara's unwavering support since our chance meeting in Kiev, in January 1961. She has kept me organized and on track with this book, as well as putting up with a house littered everywhere with books, journals and all things paper, for the last fifteen months.

As a true renaissance man, Michel has continually inspired me, as an architect, urban designer and an internationally recognized photographer and art critic. His photographic expertise has certainly enriched the book. Simply, I have been blessed, and for that I am grateful.

INTRODUCTION

The Search for a New Psychiatry -
On Becoming a Psychiatrist, Clinical Neuroscientist
and Other Fragments of Memory

For over ten years, I have been entertaining the idea of celebrating the end of my seventy years of professional and academic life by writing two new books. One book would be about my long journey across three continents to become a qualified neuroscientist and a psychiatrist, written in the re-emerging old style of literary biography. The other book would provide an analysis of the current state of psychiatry, based on my many years of practice, which has convinced me that the current state of psychiatry is failing many: patients, their doctors, their families and society at large.

As I started researching the framework for the books, I immediately realized that the information in both books considerably overlapped; inhabiting the same space and locations and dealing with many of the same people, during the same periods of time. Combining the two books and the two themes posed then as the most plausible and practical compromise, which is what I have done and what I am offering in this book. Ad priori, I felt that in writing such a book, my preferences have been to avoid the complicated and, at times, dry language of science writing. The book has been conceived, not as a science book per se, but as a book about science as perceived through my own varied experiences. I also envisaged a diverse range of readers, and, rather than limiting my writing to scientists and clinicians, I also wanted to include the many who, like me, are concerned with psychiatry and would like to know more about the origins of its failings. As a dialogue between myself and the reader, I have avoided the insertion of endless lists of references or citations, as well as the extensive use of complex population statistics. It is not that I do not trust statistics. Statistical approaches are at the core of science, and, as such, are extremely important. In this instance, my reluctance is with regard to the frequent misuse of statistics, swaying it to suit an argument, particularly, in a book like this, that relies in large part on observations and interpretations.

The book is organized into ten major parts, chronologically arranged and according to location and era. The opening, Part I, provides a brief outline of the social, economic and political climate that I grew up in, during the late 1940s and the early 1950s. As such, I consider it to be foundational, in terms of influencing my life and my career. The next few chapters deal with the origins of my initial antipathy to psychiatry, that followed my observation of a session of "Insulin Coma Therapy". On the other hand, my fascination with the ancient history of the concept and development of the "Lunatic Asylum" in Egypt, around the 8th Century, led me to include a few chapters about such early, historical advancements, up to the British occupation of Egypt in 1882. The definition of "Colonial Psychiatry" and how it delayed the development of academic psychiatry in Egypt are detailed in a separate chapter. The next few chapters record my first job as a rural physician in the remote region of Bani Ayoub, Egypt, and my very unusual experiences of fighting endemic pellagra and pellagra-madness, which initiated my early interest in the neurosciences. Following that, was my very surprising mission to Moscow for postgraduate studies, occupying several chapters and dealing with politics, ideology, science and religion, as well as personal issues, such as loneliness, love and perseverance.

My return to Cairo, after what I frequently referred to as my "expedition to Moscow" was accomplished, is sadly documented as a major disappointment. However, a life-changing and career-saving lifeline was suddenly extended to me, in the form of a post-doctoral year at one of the world's best health research institutes, in Rome. The pleasure and challenges of finally gaining control of my destiny is shared with the readers in a few chapters. The sudden Russian invasion of Czechoslovakia in the summer of 1968, all of a sudden altered my plans and intended destination, from London, England to Calgary, Canada, with a stopover for a few days in Toronto. Mysteriously, the stopover has lasted for over fifty years, as a result of an unplanned, but welcomed enroute offer from the University of Toronto.

In Toronto, my neuroscience background and clinical psychiatry came together, at last, in both extensive professional and academic roles. A number of the book's chapters focus on a few of what I consider to be my major interests and accomplishments, covering issues such as mental health systems and quality of psychiatric care, as well as broadening psychiatric outcomes, dealing with issues that matter to the person behind the psychiatric disorder, that included stress, quality of life, psychopharmacology and why some patients hate to take their anti-psychotic medications, to the degree that they would take their own life, in order to have their complaints listened to.

A major section of the book, Part IX, presents an analysis of the current state of psychiatric practice, which, regrettably, receives a failing report. It documents how psychiatry is failing many: the patients, their doctors, their families and the society at large. The book represents over seventy years of being a physician, fifty years of which were devoted to psychiatry, both professionally and academically. The book is a cry for the urgent need of a new psychiatry, before psychiatry completely loses the trust of our patients and their families, disappoints more doctors and fails society at large.

ACKNOWLEDGEMENT

In writing a book that relays such a broad scope and diverse topics, covering over seventy years of clinical and academic practice, can be a challenge. I have been fortunate to receive major assistance in coordination and editing from Ms. Pamela Walsh, whom I acknowledge for her diligence and expertise, which she has displayed while assisting with this book, as well as with previous books. Thanks, Pam, for your valuable assistance, all with good spirit and long-lasting friendship.

Cover: "The light at the end of the Tunnel"
Oil on canvas, 40" x 40"
(By the author, A.G. Awad)

PART 1

The Cairo University Years (1949 - 1956)

The Political, Social and Economic Environment I Grew Up in, in Egypt

The summer of 1949 Egypt was hot and muggy, not different from many other summers. Yet, the summer of 1949 still stands out in my mind, as it had been a very special time. A special time that defined my professional career and my life forever. That was the time of my graduation from high school and achieving a major accomplishment, being ranked among the top one hundred of about fifteen thousand graduates who competed successfully in the Egyptian national exams of that year. That guaranteed being able to choose any faculty in any university of my choice. Though my passion over the years of high school was more in literature, humanities and the arts, choosing to study medicine was a clear choice. Not only lured by practicalities of life, but I was as motivated and curious about the new medicine that had been evolving a few years earlier by the major discoveries of penicillin and other transformational antibiotics. Famous medical personalities like Anton Chekhov and Marcel Proust, who were among my favourites, made it big as writers and posed an attractive model for aspiring young people like myself.

At that time, my family lived in the large provincial city of Zagazig, about seventy kilometres north-east of Cairo in the Nile Delta, east of the Nile Rosetta branch and not far from the Suez Canal. In modern Egypt the city of Zagazig serves as the capital city of the large and prosperous Al-Sharqia Governorate. The region around Zagazig has been well recognized economically for its extensive

1

and well developed agricultural productivity. At that time, Zagazig served as the major trade centre in Egypt for cotton and maize, a non-sweet variety of corn. Additionally, in view of its proximity to the Suez Canal, and since the invasion and occupation of Egypt in 1882, many British troops frequently crossed through the region on their way to their military bases around the Suez Canal. For the same reason, Zagazig and the region around it served as the frontier for national resistance to the British occupation by nationalist groups from the left and right of the political spectrum. Historically, the region around the city of Zagazig was closely connected to ancient Egyptian civilization around the nineteenth Dynasty, when the capital of ancient Egypt was moved from Thebes to Bo Basta, a suburb of the modern city of Zagazig, locally known as Tall Basta (The Hills of Basta). The place was named after the sacred cat Bastet, which ancient Egyptians credited for protection, fertility and motherhood. Excavations in the region uncovered the largest number of mummified cats, as the region served as the burial grounds for sacred cats.

My parents moved to Zagazig in 1940, from the small town of Kaliub, less than fifteen kilometres away from Cairo, on the main railway line to Cairo, and that's where I was born.

Both my parents' extended families lived in two nearby villages, which were typical of the feudal Egyptian villages of the time, mostly dominated by a few rich land-owning families. Both my parents' families were prominent and notable Copt families, who were among the few big landowners. My father's family was noted to be more educated, with a few members having managed to achieve senior positions in the government or in the professions. Both families lived comfortably, leasing their land to the farmers who cultivated the land and were frequently in major debt, borrowing money on their crops even before the crops were harvested. A process that perpetuated living in poverty most of their life.

I attended kindergarten at a private school run by American and British nuns. By the time the family moved to Zagazig for my father to assume a more senior position, I was ready to start primary school and the Second World War was already in its second year. Though Egypt did not initially join the war, a large presence of allied troops populated large cities like Cairo, Alexandria and the Suez Canal region, creating an inflated economy. On orders from the British occupation authorities, most of the agricultural products in Egypt were redirected to the Allied war efforts, creating shortages and an inflated economy with very few Egyptians excessively benefiting from the war economy. Not surprising then that the country was paralyzed by frequent economic and political crises that led to protests and demonstrations, and also frequent changes in government that created a state of dangerous political instability. A government after government appeared to be hopelessly ineffective as the real power and authority. The authority resided with the British occupying leaders, and to a lesser extent by the King, King Faruk, and his palace functionaries. An incident in 1942 known as the "Palace Incident" rocked the country. Following a conflict between the King and the British authorities, British troops surrounded the palace in the order of the British Ambassador, Sir Miles Lampson, offering the King two choices, abdication or a change of the government to one that cooperates fully with the British authority. The King was forced, under the threat of tanks around the Palace, to compromise; a humiliating situation that further inflamed the population's discontent. Meanwhile, a small group of political activists attempted in 1942 to connect with German troops that had already reached the east border with Libya, on the mistaken assumption that the Axis occupation of Egypt could end the long battle against the British occupation. The attempt failed and led to a wave of massive arrests of the German sympathizers, which added further political upheavals to an already volatile political situation. The Prime Minister was then assassinated by a German sympathizer, to be followed by another politician, Mahmood al Nukrashi Pasha. Fortunately, the Allied forces prevailed and the war ended with their clear victory.

With departure of the many Allied forces from Egypt, the Egyptian economy plummeted, adding to the already troubled state of the economy. The opposition to the British occupation got much louder and more aggressive, sabotaging British Army installations around the Suez Canal. Such was the environment in Egypt, which was particularly noted in the city of Zagazig, at the time I started high school.

By 1947, on and off negotiations with the British Authority successfully ended in an agreement to end the presence of British troops in large Egyptian cities and regroup them only in the region of the Suez Canal. On the surface, such an agreement seemed like a victory for the nationalist sentiment, but in practice it did not squelch the opposition to the British occupation, even though it was already limited around the Suez Canal. Cities like Zagazig, close to the Suez Canal, all of the sudden became on the front line for launching Fedayeen sabotage attacks against the British garrison around the Suez Canal, attracting nationalist activists from both the radical right and left and all in between. It frequently led to some disruption of school activities, but also an increased tension in the life of the city.

To further complicate the fragile political situation, the new Israeli Prime Minister, David Ben Gurion, on May 14, 1948 announced the independence of the State of Israel, following a similar declaration the day before by the United Nations General Assembly. As the Arab Nations rejected the United Nations' partition plans, the Egyptian and other Arab nation's armies hurriedly mobilized to launch a military action against Israel, starting what became known as the "War of Israeli Independence". As happens only in royal events, the school and government workers were ordered to assemble in the Zagazig railway station and along the railway route, to cheer departing army soldiers inside the trains that were transporting them to the Sinai, on their route to fight in Palestine. I recall standing among the huge crowd that filled and overflowed the space, surrounded by classmates and all the teachers except for Mr. Chapman, the British English language teacher. Slowly the trains went by, carrying the packed soldiers who were waving passively, looking withdrawn and almost emotionless, as if unclear about where they were being taken. Most likely they were struggling with a lack of appropriate preparation that followed the rather sudden decision to enter a war. In life there are always a few live pictures that persist in memory forever and one such picture for me was that of the almost emotionless faces of the soldiers departing for the war. I am sure such a sad scene was likely one of the precursors of my later pacifist sentiments.

By now, the history of the "Israeli War of Independence" is very well known and has been reviewed over and over in multitudes of published books and many political and military war analysis. Though in the early stages of the war, the Egyptian Army seemed to do well, fighting in Gaza and Beersheeba, but such victories were quickly reversed by a crushing and humiliating defeat against more motivated and better trained and equipped Israeli army units. The bad news slowly trickled down to the Egyptian public, who had been kept mostly in the dark and were shocked and humiliated. The only Egyptian army unit that persevered courageously under Israeli siege in the Negev Desert was the unit led by the young and little-known Colonel Gamal Abd al-Nasser. It is very likely that the crushing pain of defeat and humiliation planted the seeds for the major army revolt that led to Nasser and his group of Free Officers launching their July 26, 1952 revolution, which took over the government and toppled the monarchy a bit later, radically changing the history of modern Egypt. It was a twist of fate and history that in such a humiliating defeat, a new history of Egypt was born. That was a bit of positive news, but before Nasser's Revolution to happen in 1952, the country had to go through another four years of political and economic major upheaval. With the return of the Egyptian army units to Egypt after the armistice was declared, the Moslem Brotherhood brigades that fought with the Egyptian army in Palestine, and emboldened by their strong show of fighting capabilities, started to create serious crises and put a good deal of political pressures on the government.

Regrouping and mounting several wide protests pressing for the end of the British occupation in Egypt, the Moslem Brotherhood and other radical right parties, such as "Misr al Fata" (Egypt Youth Party) and other radical socialists and a few communists, largely expanded their Fedayeen (nationalist fighters) against British troops stationed around the Suez Canal. Alarmed by the serious sabotage activities, the British authorities threatened to redeploy British troops once more in large cities. Faced with such serious British threats, the government of the time, led then by Prime Minister Mahmoud al Nukrashi, declared martial law in December 1948, and also signed a decree to outlaw the Moslem Brotherhood as an organization. In revenge, the prime minister was assassinated by a member of the banned organization at the end of December 1948. A few weeks later in February 1949, the leader of the outlawed Moslem Brotherhood, Hassan al Banna, was gunned down, very likely by an agent of the government secret services, in revenge for the assassination of the prime minister. Thousands of the outlawed members of the Moslem Brotherhood and many other radicals were arrested and many of them disappeared into jails or got deported, particularly in the case of Egyptian born foreign citizens, mostly Jewish, who populated the rather small, but influential socialist and communist movements in Egypt, such as Henry Curel, who founded the Democratic Movement for National Liberation. His communist rival, Hillal Schwartz, and Curel both were somewhat popular on university campuses as activist intellectuals were deported in 1950.

The political situation seemed to worsen by the day, inflicting massive national tensions within the seemingly harmonious relationship between Moslem and Christian communities, which got sadly shattered. Attacks on churches and Coptic-owned businesses were vicious. Churches were torched in Zagazig and other cities. The religious harmony and tolerance that was established during the 1919 national revolt, led by the nationalist Saad Zaghloul, seemed to get slowly eroded and replaced by violent extremism against foreign entities, lumping Coptic communities with them, just based on shared religion. That was the most frightening moment for Christians in Egypt. Fight or flight sadly became the modus operandi for the religious minorities, mostly Christians, who generally were represented by about ten percent of the population. Most of the Jewish Egyptian families left or were forced to leave after the 1948 war of Israeli Independence. Historically, the religious minorities had made important contributions over the years to the social, political and cultural life of Egypt. Guided by the well-known and deeply ingrained minority ethos "the need to do twice as better, in order to survive", propelled minorities to higher education and more achievements. The "golden" time for religious tolerance and harmony by sharing the popular national demands for independence in 1919, positioned prominent Copts to assume the high position of prime minister twice, early in the twentieth century and probably to the beginning of the Second World War. Boutros Ghali Pasha, was the grandfather of the later Secretary General, Boutros Boutros Ghali, who served at the United Nations, was appointed as prime minister in 1908. Similarly, another Copt, Youssef Wahba Pasha, briefly served as the prime minister of Egypt in 1919, an honour that was never repeated since then. With the successful outcome of 1919 revolution and the granting of nominal independence to Egypt in 1923, many senior positions in the government that were occupied by British or foreign nationals, became vacant according to the agreement. Many of such senior positions were quickly filled by the more qualified and better educated Christian or Jewish civil servants, particularly in senior ministries such as finance and banks. On the face of it, it appeared that most senior government positions were given to religious minority individuals favoured by the departing British authorities. Such a misperception had a triggering backlash that still continues in some form or another. The reality for those who understood the British approach to government, recognized the well-established colonial policy of convincing every party of being favoured against their opponents.

Meanwhile, the political and economic strife continued, one crisis after another, until the Black Sabbath of Grand Cairo fire on Saturday, January 26, 1952, that destroyed all foreign interests in Cairo's centre, including several foreign and Egyptian businesses owned by Jewish and Christian Coptic families, details of which are to be covered in a later chapter. It became then clear that such a tragic Cairo Black Sabbath played a major role six months later, on July 23, 1952, with the army revolution led by Colonel Nasser and his colleagues, the Free Officers, taking over the government and abandoning the monarchy. A new era of the modern history of Egypt had thus begun.

Baptism by Fire or My First Two Years of Pre-Medical on the Main Campus of Cairo University in Giza (1949-1951)

In spite of the serious political and economic upheavals, the summer of 1949 continued to be very pleasant for me and my family, proudly enjoying the happy occasion of me being the first in my extended family to enrol in medical studies. On the other hand, the joy was tempered by increasing concerns about my insistence to live independently. In the end, I prevailed and my parents reluctantly agreed. With the help of a relative in Cairo, I rented a tiny apartment on the roof of a luxurious villa in the upscale district of al Doki, about a fifteen-minute walk to Cairo University's main campus in Giza. It belonged to a wealthy physician who was also known as a conservative politician. Such a small apartment was most likely designed to accommodate their live-in servants, as it had its own separate staircase and entrance.

Walking to the campus every morning along a short-cut through the beautiful Orman Gardens in Giza was an enjoyable and easy task. The course lectures took most of the day, from 10 am to 4 pm, five days a week, with Thursday afternoons and Fridays free as the weekends. It was a relatively easy schedule that left adequate free time for other activities, such as visiting the university library and meeting with colleagues and friends, as well as sightseeing and exploring the historical landmarks of an ancient city standing side-by-side with modern structures. The main university campus was vast and impressive, with several faculties and administrative buildings nestled around.

The year 1949 was not like any other regular academic year. The humiliating defeat of the Egyptian army the year before, during the War of Israeli Independence, continued to reverberate loudly with accusations of political corruption at the highest levels. The economic state was stagnant, particularly in the countryside. The agricultural products, particularly the once highly prized Egyptian cotton, were in less demand as a result of the fierce competition from the USA and India with its cheap labour costs. The declared states of emergency or martial law were frequently followed by extensive repressive measures, including massive arrests and jailing. The assassination of the leader of the Muslim Brotherhood organization early in 1949, followed by more arrests, drove all opposition movements to operate underground. Yet on the university campus, violent demonstrations and fiery speeches continued unabated, as the university campus in Giza had become the centre for opposition, resistance and protests, not only by student groups, but also joined by labour unions and government workers.

By early 1951, the government, under massive pressure, decided to abrogate the 1936 Anglo-Egyptian Treaty that allowed British troops to continue their occupation of the region around the Suez Canal. Protests and violent demonstrations escalated almost to a boiling level, waiting to explode at any time. As a student, and for most of our class, such a divisive and volatile political environment proved to be a major challenge in how to handle such persistent pressures to join one group or another. With the uncontrolled daily protests, many students disappeared, most likely they were arrested and incarcerated in jails.

It was not that most of my class, including myself, had felt less patriotic, we were as concerned about the grim political situation that dimmed any hope for a better future. The challenge for us was to separate genuine protest from a manipulated protest, using the chaos to serve ultra radical religious or ideological aims. In essence, the challenge for me and my class was how to survive in the already narrow and tight space left between the Muslim Brotherhood on one side and the other side controlled by communists and ultra radical socialists.

Meanwhile, the end of our second year of pre-medical was quickly approaching and we had to move to the university hospital, Kasr Al Aini, for two years of medical sciences that included anatomy, physiology, biochemistry and histology, followed by three years of clinical studies.

Looking back at the two years on the main university campus in Giza, it was a great learning experience, almost like getting baptized by fire. On the other hand, the availability of some free time and the flexibility of the schedule gave us what proved to be the only free time we had during all seven years of our medical studies. It was a valuable opportunity for another type of study, exploring Cairo and its fascinating ancient history. As we quickly discovered, there was not one Cairo, but several; Islamic Cairo, the Coptic Cairo and the Jewish Cairo.

I reconnected with my old Zagazig friends, who were pursuing studies in law, political science, economics or engineering, with most of us new to Cairo and eager to explore its ancient mystical history. We managed to arrange several Friday tours to various districts of the "old Cairo" (Misr al Kadema). One of the most fascinating experiences on some Fridays was strolling through the ancient Al

Muizz Street in the heart of the Islamic quarters, where the history of Egypt since the 7th century conquest by the Arabs unfolded in a monumental and spectacular fashion. Each of the many grand mosques with their elaborate and beautiful architectural details were a representation of the various dynasties of their origin.

The cultural influences of the various dynasties, from the Abbassides, Fatimides, Mamluks and Ottoman, were on live display. The many "sabils", drinking water fountains that served people and horses, were conspicuous by their beautiful and unique Arabesque designs. The numerous sabils commemorated influential ruling families and benevolent Cairo residents. Visiting Al Muizz Street after the Friday prayers transferred one to an era, though long gone, still transcended in time through the well kept social and cultural rituals that sprang up sharply into life. Crowds strolled, ate and shopped through its many markets; the silver and gold markets, copper smiths, spice and antique markets and also many others in the nearby Al Mouski and Ghoria areas. Taking a little rest and a reprieve from the deafening noise outside, a visit to one of the grand mosques such as the Qalawoon Mosque complex or the older Al-Azhar Mosque provided unique quiet and contemplative moments.

Equally fascinating in our historical and cultural quest for knowledge and fun were our visits to the old Coptic and Jewish quarters (Misr al Kadima), with its rich and old history that goes back to the 3rd century. Among the many churches and monasteries there, the "Hanging Church" (Al Mullaga Church) stood out as the place where the Holy Family was believed to have stayed during their flight to Egypt, seeking a refuge from the tyranny of the Roman Emperor Herod. The church got its name from being suspended on the two bastions of the old Roman fortress of Babylon. With such a rich and holy history, the church used to be dilapidated and in poor structural condition. It was not for lack of funds for renovation, but was the result of seemingly deliberate neglect by successive governments for a long time. The first international tour of Tutankhamun treasures generated huge funds that were supposed to be earmarked for restoration of antiquities, but, unfortunately, none was spent on antiquities as most of the funds just joined the country's general finances. Fortunately, in recent years and with particular support from the current president, General El-Sisi, restrictions on renovations were lifted and the church seems to have been saved from neglect.

Not far from the Hanging Church, another historically important church stands; the Church of Saints Serguis and Bachus, believed to have been built in the 5th century. The church was dedicated to the two Roman army officers, Serguis and Bachus, who were martyred in Syria. Under the church, lies a cave where it is believed to be the place where the Holy Family hid. Nearby, the synagogue "Ben Ezra" has stood since the 8th century, occupying the spot of a previous church; the Saint Michael's Church. According to some accounts, a synagogue was in place prior to conversion to a church, which was destroyed by the Roman authorities. After the Arabs took over Egypt, the place was given to the Coptic community, but got destroyed again by fire around the 10th century. Early in the 12th century, the Rabbi of Jerusalem's visit to Egypt permitted the reconstruction of the synagogue to be eventually named after him, as the current Ben Ezra Synagogue. The synagogue, like other Coptic churches, survived a similar state of neglect until the peace treaty with Israel was signed in 1973, then the synagogue was renovated and restored to its original state. Visiting the nearby Gamaleya District, there was the well known "Harat al Yahud" (Jewish Street), where many Jewish families settled on arrival to Egypt many centuries ago and the small crowded houses and workshops displayed what was left of the old Jewish culture and traditions.

All in all, such unique experiences in acquainting ourselves with our ancient ancestry not only provided new knowledge, but also put us in touch with parts of ourselves that enhanced our national identity, irrespective of any identification with any organized formal religion or philosophy.

An Accidental Peek of a Live Session of Insulin Coma Therapy - My Early Antipathy to Psychiatry

As I successfully completed my two years of pre-medical science at the end of June 1951, I was lucky to be able to move to a small apartment I rented in the district of Munira, about a fifteen minute walk from the Kasr al Aini University hospital, where I would spend the next five years of my medical studies. The first two years were devoted to the study of basic clinical medical sciences that included physiology, anatomy, biochemistry and histology. The lectures at noon were followed by the anatomy dissection theatre every afternoon, using human cadavers preserved in repugnant smelling formaldehyde. The physiology lab on some mornings proved to be most entertaining, handling tiny little frogs jumping all over. The supervisor for my group was the British chairman of the department, Professor Anrep, who frequently displayed a hilarious sense of humour.

The anatomy dissection afternoons were mostly formal and frequently reflective about the life of those humans who ended as cadavers, in the service of medical training for future doctors. Professor Farag, the supervisor of my group, was a very interesting person who also taught anatomy to fine art students from the Institute of Fine Arts. He was mostly philosophical in his concept of the human body as the most beautiful model of art construction and function. Professor Derry, the Irish chairman of the Department of Anatomy, was famous for his acrobatic skills, frequently jumping up on the bench during his lectures to pose his body, as a practical demonstration of muscle groups. His lectures were frequently amusing and included historical anatomical anecdotes, such as why in the Middle Ages there were not many Christian doctors. Apparently, the church authorities prohibited the dissection of the human body, with the reason that only "God" can look at the secrets hidden in the human body. Such a preposterous excuse seemed to last until the Reformation era.

Overall, by early November of 1951, my study routine and my life in general had been quickly settled. Noticing my anatomical clay models of certain body organs that I made for study and as a hobby, Professor Farag convinced me to also pursue art, by auditing an evening art course that he delivered at the Cairo Institute of Fine Arts. I was glad to accept and, overall, it turned out to be a highly enriching experience.

One afternoon at the end of November 1951, I decided to take a short break from the formaldehyde-filled air of the dissection theatre and seek some fresh air in the gardens in front of the administration building. It faced the gate leading to the busy Kasr al-Aini Street, which was always crowded with people and the old, noisy tram lines. As I was walking along slowly, dressed in my formaldehyde- stained white coat, a youngish looking middle-aged woman dressed elegantly in the modern European style, spotted me as she disembarked from a taxi in front of the ornamented metal gate. She initially spoke in French, but quickly switched to Arabic with a very distinct Lebanese dialect. She appeared interested in the directions to the Department of Psychiatry. Since I had not yet started my clinical rotations, I offered to inquire for her.

As it turned out, there was no Department of Psychiatry, in terms of inpatient facilities, but a large outpatient clinic was in a nearby building. I offered to accompany her to that building, where we were asked by a male receptionist to wait a bit to speak to the chief psychiatry resident, since all the academic professors had left for their private clinics. Shortly, the door of a large hall opened and we moved halfway down it for the visitor to talk to the chief resident doctor. Through the semi-open door, I could not miss a quick glimpse of what was going on there; a few patients lying almost comatose on stretchers with their arms attached to intravenous tubing, and nurses, young doctors and medical students attending to them. Some of the patients were twitching violently, struggling and bizarrely gesturing, a scene that looked like a picture from hell. The chief resident apologized about being busy with sessions of insulin-induced coma therapy. He was unable to give any advice to the visitor, who identified her name as EK, who was on a brief visit to Cairo from Beirut, searching for a psychoanalyst to consult with regarding a tic condition that she had had for years. He explained that none of the psychiatry academic staff practiced psychoanalysis, but promised if he could find a name he would contact me, as the visitor was leaving for Beirut the next day.

On our way back to the gate for a taxi, the visitor was visibly disappointed. She displayed more twitching in her face, neck and shoulders, with audible vocalizations and grunting sounds. On our way back she explained that there were few psychoanalysts in Beirut, but because of her family's high political status, attending a psychiatrist for any reason was a grave stigma and a major political liability. We exchanged addresses and she left for her hotel, which she mentioned to the taxi driver as the famous Shepheard Hotel.

I returned to the anatomy dissection theatre feeling unsettled by the horrific scene of the patients receiving insulin coma therapy, but also by the very surprising and unexpected visitor. By mid-December 1951, I was given the name of a private psychoanalyst who was an Egyptian of Greek and Armenian ancestry and who was trained in France. In a few days I forwarded the information to Madam EK, who responded in a telegram, confirming the appointment date given by the psychoanalyst; Saturday, January 26, 1952, at five o'clock. She would be arriving on January 25, 1952, at midday and included an invitation for an evening dinner, as a thank you for my assistance. She concluded by reminding me that she would be staying at the Shepheard Hotel.

Meanwhile, as I was pleased that the arrangement worked out and I had been able to help, I continued to feel very unsettled about the accidental and terrifying scene of the comatose patients. I could not easily get off my mind the notion of making patients sick in order for

15

them to get better, as it did not make sense to me. It basically seemed that the cure was as bad as the illness itself. Unable to reconcile my very mixed feelings, I consoled myself by being clear about one issue, psychiatry was not going to be my field. The antipathy was so strong that at that early stage I started to worry about my future clinical rotations and how to avoid the month that I needed to go through training in psychiatry. Meantime, my life as a medical student continued and regained its regular rhythm, and once a week I juggled some time to attend Professor Farag's art course in the afternoon.

In contrast, the political scene in Cairo had been getting more tense by the day, with frequent anti-British demonstrations and more serious student protests. By early January 1952, there were sabotage attacks on the British army bases around the Suez Canal, which were mostly focused on the British army headquarters in the City of Ismailia. Serious clashes erupted around the city of Ismailia as the British army decided to demolish buildings in a few nearby villages, in an effort to clear the area that was thought to be the launching grounds for the serious sabotage attacks on the British garrison.

In an attempt to control the situation and prevent its escalation, the Egyptian government sent a unit of police auxiliary officers to be stationed at the police headquarters in the city of Ismailia. The situation further escalated by the British miscalculation of the government's intention, with accusations the police enforcement was more for the help of nationalist forces to continue their attacks on British troops. By January 25, 1952, the British troops with their heavy tanks surrounded the police headquarters in Ismailia, demanding their immediate surrender. As the demands were not met, the British general in charge gave the order to fire on the building, killing more than fifty police officers. The tragic news reached Cairo by mid-morning on January 25th, and led to huge demonstrations and protests. More national protests were organized for the next day, January 26th, which included police forces, unions, school and university students, as well as the shutting of all government offices. The tragic and sad events in the city of Ismailia seemed to touch and ignite the national anger.

As the national anger mounted by the hour, I was concerned about whether Madam EK would be able to arrive, since the Cairo airport was intermittently closed. Regardless of not receiving any news, I decided to carry on as planned and headed to the Shepheard Hotel. Surprisingly, I was told by the hotel that Madam EK had arrived late, about a couple of hours earlier. That was my first time sitting in the foyer of such a grand and extremely opulent hotel. The extra luxurious interior was hard not to miss and was highly impressive, yet the absurdity of such a contrast with the life in poor Egypt was striking and disconcerting.

After about half-an-hour of waiting, Madam EK apologized for the delay, as she worried that her delayed flight would not be allowed to land in Cairo. After a brief exchange of welcoming, and as she had already planned, after a very short walk we came to an upscale restaurant on the very upscale Alfi Bey Street, populated by the best Egyptian and European restaurants. As we settled into the well known French restaurant, La Parisienne, she gave me a small wrapped gift of a music disc, what was known at that time as a "forty-five", a vinyl record that contained the best songs by the most famous singer of the time; Nat King Cole. Soon we were engaged in discussing plans for the next day.

Madam EK seemed to be able to relax quickly and, being a heavy smoker, lit a cigarette. She opened her purse and took out a small bottle of alcohol, mentioning that she always carried it in her bag. She soaked some tissue with the alcohol and wiped all the cutlery and plates, explaining her long habit of fearing germs and not trusting even the best restaurants. An interesting observation, but not a big surprise, as I was familiar with such an obsessional cleaning urge in one of my mother's relatives. As the conversation continued, she put her lit cigarette on the ashtray, accidentally touching the tissue that was soaked in alcohol, creating a little fire that was quickly put out. Her face tics became more pronounced as she continued to apologize for her behaviour, but she was more concerned with her superstitious beliefs and interpreted it as an omen of something bad to come. I tried to reassure her as much as I could, as the dinner continued. After dinner I accompanied her to the hotel, with a plan of picking her up the next day in the early afternoon for her long awaited visit with the psychoanalyst.

I decided to walk home, which was about forty minutes, to clear my perplexed mind regarding the events of the dinner and the whole picture that Madam EK presented. It was a puzzle that I was not yet able to put together, but definitely left me curious and somewhat intrigued with what was behind such a complex picture. In a way such thoughts seemed to somewhat balance the significant antipathy that I harboured a few weeks earlier, following the accidental observation of insulin coma therapy. For a short while, I felt that neurology and behaviour could be an intriguing career prospect. Regardless, my immediate concerns shifted back to what might happen the next day with the massive and highly organized demonstrations that would include police officers and several sectors of society. A day of national anger and grief.

By mid-morning the next day, January 26th, as frequently happened in Cairo during major events, radios everywhere were up to their maximum volume, relating the progression of the demonstrations and protests that had already started to march from the university campus in Giza. They were to be joined by protesting police forces, union workers and more students, marching towards the centre of Cairo. By noon, there was ominous news that violence and the burning of foreign-owned establishments had begun, which included banks, travel agencies, luxury department stores, such as Cicurel, private clubs and the famous cinemas Metro and Rivoli. The whole commercial centre of Cairo was smouldering with fire. The smoke billowed up into the sky, covering Cairo with dark, smoky clouds.

By noon, I was alarmed and not sure what I could do. I felt panic-stricken and decided to find my way to the Shepheard Hotel in the centre of Cairo. No trams were running, as all public transportation was cancelled in order to allow all employees to join in the demonstrations and protest. There was no alternative except to walk to Ismail Pasha Square (currently named Tahrir Square). I then continued walking along Soliman Pasha Street, which proved to be an impossible task as crowds filled the streets. The air was replaced by the heavy smell of smoke coming from the many shops that were still smouldering from fire. The most luxurious furniture store, Pontermoly, was already destroyed. With great difficulty I was able to reach Mustafa Kamil Square, which was overflowing with crowds and heavy repugnant sweet smoke from the burning sugar sacks inside the famous upscale Gropi Caffe. No fire brigades, no police officers, no one seemed to be in control, like a big jungle on fire.

I zigzagged through several small streets and after a couple of hours I reached Opera Square, where the famous opera theatre stood in flames. The irony was that the building of such a luxurious venue, as well as many others like it, was built by Khedive Ismail in 1869, to entertain his celebrity guests and the royals who were attending the celebration of the opening of the Suez Canal, and was behind Egypt incurring massive international debt that eventually led to the British occupation of Egypt in 1882. As the smoke and crowds got dense, the protesters occupied the nearby Azbakyyia Gardens and beyond. I could not move any further, but from a distance I was able to catch a glimpse of the famous Shepheard Hotel, engulfed in a huge fire that destroyed what was then considered the jewel of Egyptian luxury. Built in 1841, the Shepheard Hotel became the symbol of foreign and European presence in Egypt. It frequently hosted international celebrities and kings and queens from all over the world. It served as the Allied Forces' headquarters in both world wars. It was the favourite hotel of Winston Churchill during his many visits to Egypt.

After a couple of hours of almost standing still, I was in a mixed state of fear and panic. I decided to try searching around the Azbakyyia Garden, in case some of the hotel guests were sheltering there. Finally, in the evening, the army forces were called out and a state of emergency and a curfew were declared.

I slowly walked back towards my apartment, exhausted and in despair, lamenting the huge damage that the centre of Cairo had sustained, but I was much more worried about the fate of Madam EK and whether she survived the horrible day and the tragic turn of events. As I slowly walked back, tired and dispirited, I thought several times about the little fire in the restaurant the day before and how Madam EK took it as a terrible omen. I wondered, and still do, whether it was a tragic coincidence or if it truly was an event of extra sensory perception, does such a thing really exist.

As always, life tends to continue on, regardless of misfortunes or tragedies. I resumed my studies, but was anxious to learn the fate of Madam EK. It was not until about two months later that I finally received a letter from her, briefly relating her horrific experiences on the night of January 26th. She was rescued with other guests and escorted to the Lebanese Embassy, where the next day an emergency return on a cargo ship was arranged from the city of Port Said to Cyprus and then to Beirut. Madam EK wrote about how much better she was already feeling after her horrific ordeal and that she had abandoned her plans to see a psychoanalyst, or any therapist, and was just glad to be alive. Reflecting on her letter and on the whole tragic experience, it seemed clearly that life frequently acquires its real value only through a lot of suffering.

As a corollary to such a story, while writing this chapter I asked myself why include such life experiences in a book focused on psychiatry and neurosciences? The closest answer I can figure is that it is a story about psychiatry, behaviour and neurosciences. The massive explosion of demonstrations and public protests that culminated in the grand fire during Black Sabbath can only be understood as the ultimate response of people who were treated badly for a long time, ignored and driven into a deep state of despair. A process which is not dissimilar from how an individual would respond in such situations, by feeling hopeless and helpless and becoming depressed.

From another perspective, the story of Madam EK was one of those coincidental happenings that likely added to my curiosity and interest in the neurosciences. Indeed, that story returned and came alive in my early years of psychiatry in Canada, while working with Professor Harvey Moldofsky, who had extensive clinical and academic interests in research of a condition called Tourette's syndrome or Tic disorder, which in retrospect would have been the correct diagnosis of Madam EK's clinical condition.

An Unsettling Visit to the Old Abbassyia Mental Asylum - Connecting the Present with the Ancient Colonial Past

A visit to the old Abbassyia Mental Asylum was arranged for one afternoon in April of 1954, as part of our psychiatry course. The psychiatry core lecture series at the Kasr al Aini Hospital proved to be a bit dull and hardly inspiring. Most of the teaching was organized in the language of psychoanalytic concepts and theories, using theoretical jargon that was unfamiliar to many of us. There was little history and much less on the new and evolving psychopharmacology developments that had been emanating rapidly from France, Canada and the US since the early 1950s. So, the anticipation of the visit to the Abbassyia Asylum was awaited with some curiosity and the hope for observing and learning something different.

Buses were prearranged to take the class to the Abbassyia District, where the asylum was located. It was not far from the Ataba Square, considered to be the central point in Cairo where all the tramway lines covering the city began and ended. The trip took more than an hour, slowly moving along the narrow and congested streets. I cannot imagine how long such a trip would take nowadays, in the present Cairo of about twenty million people, compared to the Cairo of four to five million in 1954.

As we disembarked in front of the hospital, we were quickly ushered in through a wide iron gate that still retained some of its palatial past. The original building of the hospital was known as the Red Palace and was built by Khedive Ismail, to host some of his royal and celebrity guests attending the lavish ceremonies held during the opening of the Suez Canal in 1869. For some reason, the Red Palace was never used and remained empty until it was completely destroyed by a major fire in 1878, excluding the gates. A few years later, the Red Palace was rebuilt to its original state by Khedive Tawfiq, the son of Ismail, who succeeded his deposed father. Once more the palace remained empty, until 1884, two years after the British occupation of Egypt began, when it was converted into a mental asylum. The few patients who were still living in the dilapidated and deteriorated Cairo Lunatic Asylum, in the District of Boulaq, got transferred to the new building in the Abbassyia District.

Walking through the gates to the vast front garden of the asylum, we saw a large round fountain that no longer functioned, with many patients sitting or standing on its ledge, shouting and screaming. Some patients were bizarrely gesturing, as if delivering rambling speeches. Others were reciting some religious texts and dressed in odd ceremonial attire. The garden was full of people who were poorly dressed or barely dressed at all. One person, who wore the full military attire of Napoleon Bonaparte and spoke fluent French, kept following us. The crowd was made up entirely of men, as the women were kept segregated in a different location. The noise was deafening and in no time at all we were swamped by the crowd around us, asking for cigarettes and money, but on the whole they were non-violent.

We eventually were rescued by the staff, who directed us to a large hall for a welcome speech by the Director (no longer using the title of Superintendent), whose name I still remember; Dr. Wagdi. He impressed us with his knowledge and sense of history, updating us with the ongoing reforms to transfer the old asylum into a modern psychiatric hospital. After a quick tour of the truly overcrowded wards, we assembled in a lecture theatre to listen to presentations by the senior Egyptian psychiatrists in charge of the various programs.

We learned that the population of the hospital patients included a mix of psychiatric cases over the years, the majority of whom had been diagnosed as suffering from schizophrenia or an intractable manic-depressive condition. A number of patients were suffering from all types of dementia, including a few with pellagra-induced dementia, caused by a lack of niacin. We were told about a few patients who had been admitted at a young age and were eventually abandoned by their families. With nowhere else to go, some of them had lived most of their life in the institution. Other patients with no serious mental disorder were admitted through the lax old mental health laws, following squabbles within wealthy families about inheritance, or just to get rid of them to avoid public embarrassment and social shame. This was somewhat consistent with what the French social scientist, Michel Foucault, had extensively written about regarding incarceration in mental hospitals as an exercise of power for the purpose of exclusion. We were relieved to learn that such practices had stopped and were replaced by clearly defined admission criteria.

Two of the presentations were detailed and proved to be most interesting, attracting the full attention of the class. The first was a snapshot of the history of mental health care, going back to the early 8th and 9th centuries in Cairo, during the Tulumid and Abbasid ruling era. A hospital was developed then that included a wing for mental health care, at a time when Western countries were still struggling in the dark ages, awaiting reforms. The other impressive presentation was the parallel story taking place at that time in Paris, France, about the discovery of the first specific antipsychotic, chlorpromazine, and the rise of the era of new psychopharmacology.

Early Roots of Mental Health Care in Egypt

In 872 CE, a bimaristan (the Persian name for a hospital) was built by the ruler Ahmad Ibn Tulun in Fastat, the location of where the city of Cairo was subsequently developed. The bimaristan was one of the earliest known concepts of a hospital that included care of the mentally ill. The Tulun bimaristan served as a medical and social facility that provided free medications and included two bathhouses, one for women and another for men. It also included a library and a large stack of books. A special wing was dedicated for the treatment of the "insane".

Years later, in 1283, another bimaristan was built by the Mamluk ruler, Sultan Qalawoon, and named The Mansuri Maristan (hospital). The Qalawoon hospital was more specialized and included mental health services. It is interesting to note that the Persian word "maristan" is still in use in modern Egypt, denoting a madhouse or describing situations that are mostly chaotic. Over time, the bimaristan was renamed as the Cairo Lunatic Asylum, which continued till about the year 1857. It was already in a state of neglect and deterioration that necessitated the transfer of the remaining patients to a warehouse in the District of Boulaq, which turned out to be in equally poor shape. Nevertheless, the Boulaq facility continued to exist until 1884, two years after the British occupation of Egypt, when patients were transferred to the Red Palace, Abbassyia District, to begin what became known as the Abbassyia Mental Asylum.

Meanwhile, and separately from the historical development of the Abbassyia Mental Asylum, in the year 1827, during the era of the Ottoman reformer and ruler, Mohamad Ali, a large military medical facility was built in the town of Abu Zaable, not far from Cairo, to serve Mohamad Ali's expanding army in its extensive military conquests. The hospital was designed and managed by his close French friend and medical advisor, Antoine Barthelemy Klott, known as Klot Bey. Years later, after the military garrison relocated from Abu Zaable, the hospital and the attached newly developed medical school were moved to Cairo, inhabiting an old palace on the banks of the Nile, that belonged to the wealthy Al Aini family. Over time, the new hospital grew rapidly to become the largest health facility in the Middle East.

With the opening of the new Cairo University in 1925, the Kasr al Aini Hospital, as it became known, served as the university hospital, at the centre of the newly founded medical faculty. Compared to other well established main medical departments, Psychiatry was late in its development as it was established in 1938. As discussed in a later chapter, the colonial British authorities in Egypt had deliberately delayed all attempts for the development of academic psychiatry in Egypt. That meant that the new academic Department of Psychiatry at Cairo University had to do a lot of catching up, in an era when the field of psychiatry was itself going through a major transformation from the dominant, but waning, psychoanalytic influence to the modern era of psychiatry and neurobiology.

During my time as a medical student in the early 1950s, the Department of Psychiatry was basically eclectic in its concepts and practices, and heavily invested in biological treatments. Psychotherapy was practiced, but mostly in private clinics. A few attempts to change the focus of psychotherapy into a type of Islamic Sharia-based therapy did not garner much support, for fear of cutting off Egyptian psychiatry from the rapidly expanding international field.

1954: The Year that Ushered in a Psychiatric Revolution

By the end of 1954, I had completed my psychiatry training that included the course lectures, four weeks of clinical observations in the psychiatric outpatient clinics and a visit to the Abbassyia Psychiatric Hospital, which was rather disturbing, but most informative about the challenges facing the science and practice of psychiatry. I have to admit, psychiatry was never my first career choice. Therapeutic approaches on the whole appeared as crude, clumsy and not that effective. The science looked shaky and was mostly absent. Though significant reforms were introduced by the time of our visit in 1954, the conditions there were far from adequate or appropriate, and they continuously struggled with unacceptable overcrowding. To expect extra funding and more radical reforms proved to be beyond possible at that time.

Only two years after the 1952 revolution, the country was politically unstable and having to deal with one crisis after another. Political conflicts between Nasser and President Naguib complicated matters and ended with the removal and house arrest of Naguib, with Nasser assuming the position of Prime Minister. Shortly after, an assassination attempt of Nasser failed, but, as is usual following such events, there were massive arrests and jailing of members of the Moslem Brotherhood who were implicated in the failed assassination attempt. Demonstrations and protests filled Cairo and other big cities, threatening the seemingly fragile stability that followed the 1952 revolution. The threat extended to the possible closure of schools and universities, which became seriously embroiled in the new wave of protests.

Among the prevailing and mounting tensions, the only positive event was the imminent conclusion of the British occupation, as had been negotiated between the Egyptian and British governments. Unfortunately, before the last British army unit had left Egypt a major crisis erupted, known now as the "Lavon Incident". It involved the arrest of an Israeli ring, organized by the Mossad, the Israeli Secret Service, to sabotage some of the British and US diplomatic buildings, in an effort to create chaos and to convince the British not to leave, as agreed upon, and to continue their occupation. With the failure of the plot, which apparently was hatched without the knowledge of the Israeli government, Mr. Lavon was forced to resign as the Israeli Defence Minister.

While political tensions were mounting by the day, another interesting story was playing out in Paris, France; the new discovery of chlorpromazine, ushering in a revolution that changed the face and practice of psychiatry for years to come. It was very welcome and exciting news that seemed somehow to lighten up the disappointment we had encountered over the years with psychiatry, from the somewhat barbaric insulin coma treatment to the chaotic overcrowding in the Abbassyia Psychiatric Hospital.

RP4680 – The Molecule that Changed the Face and Practice of Psychiatry

The summer of 1940 marked the second year of the Second World War and the rapidly escalating savage marine sea battles, including a French destroyer sunk by a German torpedo boat. On the destroyer was a French military doctor, Henry Laborit, who was seriously injured, but rescued in the Channel Sea. To recover, he was sent to Senegal, a French colony in Africa at that time. During his slow recovery, he gradually started to practice as a surgeon. Discouraged by the frequent post-operative surgical fatalities, he seriously wondered if it was caused by a state of surgical shock, not dissimilar from the state of "shell shock" that was frequently observed during the First World War. Dr. Laborit developed a strong belief that such states were likely related to the release into the blood of the chemical "histamine" from injured body tissues during surgery. With his interest in medications, he developed several theories that formed the basis of developing a number of medication cocktails, in an attempt to protect against the development of post-surgical shock, but with little or no success.

Dr. Laborit persisted and in his efforts to find the right medications, he contacted the major French pharmaceutical company, Rhone Poulanc. He inquired whether the company may have a substance that would serve as a histamine blocker, knowing the company's major interest in the development of anti-allergy medications. The company quickly obliged, particularly as Rhone Poulanc had already identified a possible candidate, RP4680, which the company decided not to develop, as a result of its serious sedating side-effects.

Eventually moving to Paris, Dr. Laborit joined the military hospital, Val-de-Grace, in Paris. Having in his possession the RP6480 substance that Rhone-Poulanc had provided in 1951, he sought collaboration with a colleague, Pierre Huguant, who was knowledgeable about medications and was also a surgeon and anaesthetist. The timing seemed to be perfect, as the era of big pharma was under way and in full swing, developing all kinds of medications for anxiety and allergies. The definitive point came after observations from a small clinical trial that proved RP6480 possessed unique pharmacological properties, clearly calming patients while they continued to be awake. That was the long awaited moment that led to establishing contact with Dr. Pierre Deneker, a colleague at St. Anne Psychiatric Hospital, the largest psychiatric hospital in Paris. Through Dr. Deneker, contact was established with Dr. Jean Delay, who was well known for his interest in neurobiology, as well as being a strong critic of psychoanalytic theories and concepts. As the saying goes, the rest is history. More clinical trials were conducted in Europe and North America. In Canada, they were led by Professor Hanz Lehman in Montreal, and by several other prominent psychiatrists in the US. In no time, this major discovery swept through Europe and the Americas, ushering in the new era of modern psychopharmacology. A much-detailed account about the discovery of Chlorpromazine is included in the recently published excellent book "Ten Drugs: How Plants, Powders and Pills Shaped the History of Medicine, by Thomas Hager".

Nothing more underscored the significant evolving and prominent new psychopharmacology revolution than what occurred at the Second International Congress of Psychiatry, which was to be held in Zurich, Switzerland on September 2-4, 1957, chaired by Professor Nathan Kline, the Director of Research at the Rockland State Hospital in Orangeburg, New York. The painstakingly put together program, prepared in advance, was to be pre-empted to make room for the rapidly evolving psychopharmacology presentations by many well known psychiatrists, who seemed to carry the mantel of progress through the next twenty to thirty years. Indeed, a remarkable story unfolded that not only changed psychiatric practices, but also added respectability to the role of the psychiatrist as a medical specialist, as well as an academician and neuroscientist. As frequently happens in many transformational developments, an unintended downside to the chlorpromazine success story was the precipitous discharge of chronic psychiatric patients, who were to receive treatments as outpatients in communities that were not welcoming nor prepared to receive them. Unfortunately, the hasty discharge of long-term residents of the mental asylums in the early phases of what is now known as the "de-institutionalization movement" ended in creating new mental asylums in the community, on the streets and in correctional facilities.

Nevertheless, the discovery of chlorpromazine had been a story of major success that at least opened the door a little bit to, hopefully, unlock the mysteries behind devastating major mental illnesses, particularly in schizophrenia. It also provided a treatment better than any previous medications, albeit imperfect, in terms of the wide range of side-effects and not being fully effective for the broad range of symptomatology.

Colonial Psychiatry and How it Deliberately Delayed the Development of Academic Psychiatry in Egypt

In September 1882, the British troops assembled on board the British navy ships surrounding the port of the city of Alexandria and started their bombardment of the city, launching their invasion and ultimately their occupation that lasted for the next seventy-two years, until 1954.

In the few years preceding the British occupation, Egypt was going through serious economic and political upheavals. The staggering and massive foreign debt incurred by Khedive Ismail to pay for his extravagant and reckless spending, hosting the many kings, queens and celebrities invited to attend the celebrations marking the opening of the Suez Canal in 1869. Such huge foreign debt created high anxiety and serious concerns among European banks and other foreign debtors. In 1875, Khedive Ismail was forced to sell Egypt's shares in the Suez Canal Company to the British government. In practice, such a transaction allowed the British government to share control of the Suez Canal with the French government. Meanwhile, Egypt's finances were put under international control and required a foreign European representative to be appointed as a cabinet minister.

The increasing discontent among Egyptians about the take-over of the government by foreigners and foreign powers, had led concerned Egyptian nationalists to group under a new party; Hisb Al Watani (National Party), which attracted prominent Egyptians and discontented army officers. The political chaos soon led to the deposition of Khedive Ismail and his son, Tawfiq to succeed him. By 1881, the discontent among army officers led to serious protests over several broad issues related to changes in conscription, pay and promotions.

Meanwhile, the country was struggling with a serious drought that devastated the crops and the country. A number of concerned army officers, under the leadership of Colonel Urabi, seized the opportunity and staged a mutiny that ended with the appointment of Colonel Urabi as the Minister of War. Such a turn of events seemed to worry both the British and French authorities, who issued a stern protest and threat. The British navy ships were ordered to sail towards the port of Alexandria and, once in place in September 1882, bombardment of the city started, allowing the British troops to land and begin their march towards the Suez Canal. Their advance was initially halted by Colonel Urabi's Egyptian army units in the town of Kafr al-Dawar, but with new British enforcement from the Alexandria British garrison, aided by their new heavy tanks, the British troops continued their advance, crossing the Nile delta and reaching the town of Tal al Kabir, not far from the Suez Canal where the decisive battle defeating Urabi's units took place. The Egyptian resistance was crushed and Urabi was captured and eventually exiled to the British colony of Ceylon. Though Colonel Urabi and his poorly equipped Egyptian army units were defeated, by all accounts of several historians, the Tal al Kabir battle had been considered as the first courageous attempt to oppose the British occupation of Egypt.

Consolidating their power and authority, the British occupation authorities influenced and controlled all aspects of Egyptian life. Initially, the British government justified the occupation of Egypt as helping the financial reorganization of the massive Egyptian debt and return Egypt to a state of solvency. Shortly afterwards, with the help of the British propaganda, the aim of the occupation was declared as the modernization of a backward country and the protection of minority groups and other foreigners. In essence, the occupation was presented as a "gift" to Egypt, for the purpose of civilizing Egyptians and bringing them up to the level of western civilization. The message that the colonial authorities had propagated to pacify the population in their colonies, was that the occupation forces would help to develop local health and educational systems where none existed before. Except, in Egypt such a message would not be believed, as at that time there were existing health and educational systems that had already been in place for a very long time, when western countries were struggling to find their way out of the Middle Ages. An illustration of this historical fact is the concept of a hospital and a health care system that had existed in Cairo since the year 872 CE, when the Ibn Tulun bimaristan was opened. A more recent example is during the era of the reformer Ottoman ruler, Muhammad Ali, when a military hospital and the first secular medical school were established in 1825, in the town of Abu Zaabel, near Cairo. Similarly, in the same era, the Ottoman ruler, Muhammad Ali, established a school education system that benefited from the educational French push, initiated by the short-lived French Expedition and led by Napoleon Bonaparte in 1798 to 1801.

Though the British occupation authorities in Egypt could not fully claim to have established new health and educational systems, they certainly introduced badly needed improvements to old and deteriorated systems. The one area that did fit their usual claim was the horrible state of the mental asylums and mental health care, that quickly became the major focus of the British reforms. It is of interest that the choice of mental asylums and mental health care was the central focus of reforms, and took place at a time when the concept of the mental asylum in Great Britain was the subject of violent and heated debates between reformers, mostly lay people, fiercely opposed by groups of the medical elite.

At that time, interestingly enough, there was no body of science to back one group or another, particularly when it came to the etiology and effective treatments of mental disorders. The one issue that came out clearly and was accepted by all parties, was the vague concept of "moral therapy", which provided a good starting point for the mental health reforms offered by the colonial British authorities to their colonies. Lacking a scientific base, the British colonial powers were convinced that by offering a clean and sanitary place, orderly and appropriately managed, it would deliver the desired moral therapy.

And that was what the colonial authorities offered, using medicine and medical personnel as a critical tool in the process of colonization. In other words, medicine and medical persons had to serve a political agenda as Imperial agents for control in the colonies.

In 1884, two years after the invasion and occupation of Egypt, the Abbassyia Mental Asylum was resurrected, by moving whatever patients were left in the overcrowded and terribly deteriorated warehouse, the Cairo Lunatic Asylum in the District of Boulaq, to the restored Red Palace in the District of Abbassyia. The Red Palace, as discussed in an earlier chapter, was originally built by Khedive Ismail in 1869, to guest the many international celebrities on the occasion of the opening of the Suez Canal. It was never used, destroyed by fire, then rebuilt by Ismail's son, Khedive Tawfiq, but once more was abandoned. The move to Abbassyia was followed by recruitment of more staff and the enhancement of the very low budgets. Doctors were imported from Great Britain and other countries, such as France, Italy and Germany. A much firmer management system was also put in place.

In essence, the mental asylum in Cairo became one of the important faces of colonialism and, as such, it was presented as one of the few benefits and justification for the occupation. Through such a process of reforms, the British colonial power managed successfully to carve out mental health and the mental asylum as their area of reform and expertise, fully managed and controlled by the British authorities and separate from the state of governmental bodies.

Though the British colonial authorities had clearly provided a much-enhanced management of the asylum, no science was introduced, except perhaps for the detailed documentation of psychiatric symptoms and some very early efforts in attempting to classify diseases, not based on reliable or verified psychopathologies, but more so on economics and social class. However, some of the early improvements were noted by Cambridge University in 1910, in their acceptance of training at the Abbassyia Mental Asylum as meeting the requirement for a Cambridge University Psychiatry Diploma.

Unfortunately, with the pressing budgetary limitations and in the absence of new and effective therapeutic tools, beyond electric shock therapy or insulin induced coma, overcrowding and deterioration was a matter of time. A "revolving door" approach became the norm. The overcrowding managed to create significant pressures and another asylum was built in the nearby town of Khanka. The new Khanka Mental Asylum introduced a class and a disease-based administrative system by which severely ill patients were admitted to Abbassyia, as well as foreigners and wealthy, paying Egyptians.

Since 1884, the Abbassyia Mental Asylum was managed by a succession of British superintendents, the last of them and the longest serving was Dr. John Warnock, who served from 1895 to 1923, and had been credited by both British and Egyptian authorities for the significant improvements he introduced in the management and organization of care for the mentally ill. Though he did not introduce significant science, except for the systematic clinical observations related to "pellagra madness" and states of substance abuse specifically related to hashish consumption, Dr. Warnock had left a significant structure embodied in the concept of the mental asylum. What emerged clearly from such a concept had been the confirmation of the mental asylum as the "home" for psychiatry becoming recognized as a medical field and defining the role of the psychiatrist as a medical specialist. Dr. Warnock finally had to vacate his superintendent position in 1923, the year British authorities offered a nominal independence to Egypt, that guaranteed all government senior positions were to be managed and under Egyptian control.

With such important accomplishments, how then was it that colonial psychiatry was instrumental in delaying the development of academic psychiatry in Egypt? It was clear that such a delay was not by chance or extreme circumstances, but was a deliberate colonial approach in the early years of the British occupation in order to promote British superiority in knowledge, with the clear recognition that knowledge was power. Such a point was already demonstrated in the British efficiency of management. This calculated approach, directly or indirectly, propagated the notion that Egyptians were backward and could not be trusted. For Egyptian medical students to be able to practice upon graduation, they were required to be granted a diploma that was frequently denied, leaving medical practice wide open for foreign doctors who could practice without a diploma. One of the avenues open for Egyptian medical graduates was to seek employment in the mental asylum, where most of the senior positions were occupied by British or foreign doctors. At the same time, there existed a strong organized opposition to specialization in general, that was vocal even in Great Britain. In Egypt, an additional excuse raised by the British authorities pertained to the poor teaching methods at Cairo University, a process that stalled the prospect of specialization for a long time, leaving Egyptian medical graduates with the only option that was open; practising as general practitioners.

It wasn't until the year 1889, when the Dean of the medical school at Cairo University was replaced by Professor Keatings, a much fairer British educator who allowed Egyptian graduates to enrol in post-graduate training courses, including the recognized training program at the Abbassyia Mental Asylum. Obviously, one could not dismiss easily that among the motives for such a discriminating approach was the issue of control, retaining power and limiting the lucrative medical practice among foreign doctors. On the other hand, as a silver lining, such unacceptable discrimination unintentionally ended in a major gain, by strengthening the concept of the asylum and adding to it an academic medical dimension that provided credibility to the role of the psychiatrist as a clinician and a specialist.

Fast forward to the present time, the Abbassyia Mental Asylum continues, but has changed in function and name, to become a modern psychiatric hospital. The old and antiquated mental health laws had been reformed in 2009, allowing for significant expansion of services to include a large community-based program extending beyond its ancient and historic walls. The reformed Abbassyia Psychiatric Hospital has become an attractive training site, building on its remarkable and resilient historical details, from the era of the Cairo Lunatic Asylum to its present modern status as a psychiatric hospital.

In writing this chapter about colonial psychiatry in Egypt, I asked myself several times why I would include a chapter about psychiatry in a far away country, while my main intention has been to write about psychiatry in Canada. I believe the information about colonial psychiatry in Egypt is how psychiatric practices were shaped by British colonial thinking, and, in reality, is not far away from the reality of what happened in Canada or in countries that served at one time or another as a member of the colonial British Imperial powers. In deconstructing colonial psychiatry, as practised in Egypt or Canada or in other British colonies, such a process sheds light not only on historical developments in the colonies, but also presents itself as the historical development of the field of psychiatry itself.

The 1956 Suez Canal Crisis – Graduation Delayed

As we entered the year of 1956, our year of graduation in December, we started slowly to breath a sigh of relief after seven years of demanding studies. Hope trickled down slowly, mixed with a wide range of emotions and feeling that the worst was already over. There was a general feeling of accomplishment and a light at the end of the tunnel, but also with feelings of the anticipated loss of the comradely and collegial support that we enjoyed within our small group that had moved together as one team over the five years of clinical rotations. It was almost like a state of advance mourning of a collective personal relationship, that carried all of us to the end. Names that I still remember; Michael, Moukhtar, Afaf, Fathy, Farid, Wahib, Rose, Moufeed, Fauzia, Mounir and Edward were among many others who for seven years served as key members of our alternative families.

Meanwhile, it was time to start seriously thinking and preparing for future plans. Few in our class were keen and aspired to pursue an academic career after completion of the obligatory training year as a "house officer", the British equivalent of an internship. I harboured the same interest. Yet, my interests were tempered by the uneasy realization of how difficult it would be at that time for minority graduates to compete on an equal footing for the few specialized junior academic positions that were available. A number of specialized programs were in high interest and demand, but were generally closed to minority graduates. It happened that many of such programs were historically developed or long led by well-known names from minority groups, such as obstetrics and gynecology, urology, surgery, etc. A good number of my classmates appeared intended for private practice or for a position in the health units of the Ministry of Health.

Surprisingly, not a small group was opting to join the army medical corp, lured by the generous pay and the high status of the military that was elevated by President Nasser after being elected as president in 1955, after the overwhelming approval of his constitutional reforms in an already popular referendum. Another small group, mostly from religious minorities, Copts and the very few Jews left, started preparing applications for post-graduate training mostly in the United Kingdom in London or Edinburgh, as well as various academic hospitals in the US. I did the same and got accepted in both London and Edinburgh, as well as at the Good Samaritan Hospital in Cincinnati, Ohio, which in advance I knew that going to the US in the future could never be my first priority for several reasons, including, regrettably, the ongoing and violent unrest about the fight for civil rights. Politically, the relationship between the US and Egypt was also strained and spiralling quickly down. The intent of President

Nasser to turn to the Soviet block for procuring military arms that had been denied by the west, as well as his clear tilt towards a socialistic future path, infuriated the US and western countries. The last straw was the abrupt decline of the US and Britain to support the financing of the High Dam, that had been earlier approved by the International Bank for Reconstruction and Development, early in 1956. What infuriated President Nasser at that time, apart from the issue of national pride and feeling insulted, he was under significant political and economic pressure to address the urgent issue of serious economic inequality between the countryside of Egypt and the urban population of the cities, on the background of an already massive population explosion.

In July 1956, during a fiery speech in Alexandria, President Nasser declared the nationalization of the Suez Canal, in order to use the revenues from the canal to finance the High Dam project. After many failed negotiations and mounting international tension, Britain and France orchestrated a secret deal with Israel to invade Egypt and get control of the Suez Canal. On October 29, 1956, Israel invaded Egypt through the Sinai and advanced towards the Suez Canal. Meanwhile, the British and French air forces bombarded the city of Port Said, at the Mediterranean opening of the Canal, destroying and sinking a few ships in the canal. The resulting international crisis blew back in the face of the invaders. The US, not being consulted, asked for an immediate cease fire and withdrawal of the invading troops. The British parliament was equally furious for not being informed by Prime Minister Anthony Eden. In the end, and after a lot of political manoeuvring, the crisis was settled and Egypt regained full control of the Suez Canal after compensating the foreign shareholders.

Obviously, during October and November, as the war and the crisis played out, schools and universities were closed, and there went our graduation in December, which was delayed eventually to January 1957. The subdued graduation ceremonies were conducted with a sigh of relief for us, but with a deep sense of sorrow for the destruction of the city of Port Said and the loss of many lives, as the price for regaining the ownership of the Suez Canal.

In no time, the obligatory year of training as a house officer commenced at the end of January 1957. We were provided with full-time lodging and complementary meals, residing in a comfortable building next to the administrative central building in the new Kasr al-Aini Hospital. I had to vacate my rented apartment and say goodbye to Mr. F. N., the owner of the building, whom I found that he and his family were in a state of fear and panic, like all the remaining Jewish families who stayed in Egypt after the 1948 Jewish exodus. For him, and I am sure included his family, it was a very sad moment for someone who had to dislocate through no individual fault of his own, but as a collective revenge for the faults and political arrogance of others. Similarly, all French and British subjects were forced to leave the country and their properties and businesses were confiscated.

What that meant for me, personally, was that in such a hostile environment, my chances of going to London for post-graduate training became almost impossible. My application to the National Government Commission for Studies Abroad, asking for a bursary in support of studies in London, seemed to languish somewhere in a large file, along with hundreds and hundreds of other applications to the Commission's central office, located in the mega government building; the "Mogmeh" (the Grouping) in the current Tahrir Square.

By October 1957, and getting closer to the end of my year as a house officer in January 1958, I decided to accept a position as a rural physician in a remote region of Egypt, very close to the city of Zagazig, where my parents were still living. So many years later, I'm still not sure whether my decision to serve the remote region of Bani Ayoub was the comforting notion of living with my parents and family, after so many years of living on my own. Decisions were made, my mind was clearly set, and what remained was a couple of weeks to join my family in Zagazig to deal with the logistical issues of starting my first independent job.

On my way back to Zagazig, I decided to make a stopover for a few days in the village of Sendyon, which I had not visited since the death of my grandparents a few years before. One of my motivations for the visit was my curiosity about what was going on there, but also my deep interest to learn what happened to the several ancient texts about ancient folk medicine in my grandparent's library, which I used to enjoy reading during my summer holidays. I was particularly interested in an ancient book that was a handwritten copy on leather. It was written by Dawud Ben Omer al-Antaki (David of Antioch) and was popularly known by the title "Dawud Prescriptions", written in Arabic several years before his death in 1599. Dawud al-Antaki was a well-known physician and pharmacist who was born in Persia, but lived all his life in Cairo as a blind physician.

In fact, the book was two books together. The main book, by al-Antaki, who was known and famed as a physician and pharmacist in his time of the golden Arab science, was printed inside an outlined box. Outside of the box, in the margins, another book was written by one of his students and dealt with the medical and mental information about how to clear the mind, sharpen the memory and improve moods. What intrigued me every time I had the opportunity to read the al-Antaki's book was that in such a very early period, several conditions were almost correctly described as we know them in modern times, including how to be treated. An example I still remember well is about alopecia and hair loss, and the recommended treatment was with tar paste covering the scalp. Tar preparations, surprisingly, were still in some use during my medical school years, centuries later.

One of the most fascinating parts of the book was a chapter about numerology, which I believe is still practiced in Egypt, India and other countries. Numerology is about the study of numbers and, in many ways, is similar to astrology. It is based on the notion that the universe is a complex system that can get broken down and left out from its basic elements. Numerology is about the numbers that can help in the understanding of the individual world of every person. Numerology had its origins in ancient Egypt and Babylon and then migrated to China and the Greek and Roman Empires. Aspects of numerology were described in a number of Hebrew ancient texts. According to one Jewish historian, forms of numerology have survived to the present time in Judaic practices, as certain numbers continued to acquire a special significance for certain states and events, such as pleasure, loss and grief, etc.

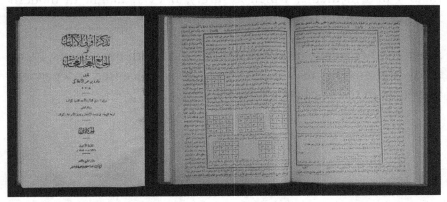

Pictures of three pages from *al-Antaki*, a medical textbook dated 1599

In Egypt, numerology acquired a magical healing power, particularly in the countryside. The knowledgeable healer and a numerologist generally composed the magic numbers for the person, which was written on a folded piece of paper and was to be worn in the armpit or around the neck, following a particular ritual. Obviously, any little benefit that occurred was related to the power of suggestion and a very strong desire to get better. This is what likely attracted my attention initially, as an early effort to exploit the therapeutic value of a powerful placebo. Nowadays, leaving aside the charlatan aspect of numerology, the science of numbers has acquired major importance and holds wide respectability, as in mathematics.

Sadly I could not find the book or any other books where my grandparents kept their collection of old books. I believe such a valuable library got lost among the squabbles and endless litigation among my relatives; the inheritors. Fortunately, a few years later I discovered that two copies of the al-Antaki Prescriptions were secured, one in the British Museum Library in London and the other in the Egyptian National Library in Cairo. I was told not long after, the Egyptian National Library was planning to reprint five-hundred copies of the book and charging five-hundred dollars each., for the use of academic scholars and medical historians. I have been fortunate to get a copy, considering my deep interest in ancient history and medicine, which is rarely, if ever, taught in modern medical schools.

After another couple of weeks of relaxation with my parents, I was ready and anxious to start my first job as a licensed independent physician in the nearby Bani Ayoub region.

PART II

My First Job – The Bani Ayoub Years (1958 – 1961)

The First Day in Bani Ayoub – Wednesday, March 7, 1958

A short trip by regular bus from the city of Zagazig to the town of Abu Hamad, the closest town to the village of Bani Ayoub, took about forty minutes, stopping often to pick up passengers from the string of small towns and villages en route. A prearranged taxi was waiting for me, which would drive me to Bani Ayoub and return me in the afternoon. The trip was short, for a distance of less than ten kilometres. The driver was friendly and in twenty minutes gave me a short history of the region around Bani Ayoub, which stretched along the edges of the desert that extended east, to the west bank of the Suez Canal.

Bani Ayoub and the string of villages and "ezbas" (small family estates) surrounding Bani Ayoub, were basically settlements created decades earlier by the government for the nomadic Bedouins who moved around in the desert. The government move was a response to the serious concerns of the British army authorities that occupied a large swath of desert land around the Suez Canal. The British army commander in the region was complaining, with added threats, because of the frequent thefts and sabotage against the British army garrison and its many military installations in the Suez Canal region. The amicable old driver did not forget to remind me of the courageous fight by Colonel Urabi's Egyptian units in 1882, against the well equipped British army and the final defeat of the Urabi units in the nearby town of Tall al Kabir, about twenty kilometres from Bani Ayoub.

As we travelled along the country road, most of it unpaved, we stopped at a narrow dirt lane in the middle of green maize fields (a sort of hardy non-sweet corn). I was told the road was a shortcut to the hospital, forgoing a longer walk through the village. A small group of people warmly welcomed me, which included a few of the hospital staff, the "omda" (mayor) of Bani Ayoub, the school principal and only teacher of the local elementary school, the "saraf" (financial comptroller and tax collector), as well as "Sheik al Ghafara" (Chief of the local guardsmen) and a donkey with its back covered by colourful Bedouin woven skirts. The omda insisted I ride the donkey to the hospital, which was less than a ten-minute walk away. The morning was sunny and warm, and a few people in the welcoming group carried umbrellas for my protection from the sun. As much as the welcoming party tried to have me take the donkey ride, I adamantly declined the kind offer, as I thought strongly of how hilarious it would be entering the hospital on my first day, riding a donkey. Up to the present day, the thought of me riding the donkey and the people following me with their umbrellas, always makes me smile and brings interesting memories with it, re-imagining myself as Don Quixote, riding a donkey in a procession to save the poor people of Bani Ayoub.

Along the narrow dirt lane there were a few scattered mud brick houses, more like huts rather than houses. As we approached closer to a small wooden bridge over a narrow canal, which I was told was the only source of fresh water for irrigation purposes, I quickly noticed an emaciated old-looking person sitting in front of a tiny house, leaning his back against the front wall. His face and his bare legs were covered by dark brownish clusters and rough crusts and blotches. He appeared stuporous or in a daze and did not respond to me waving and saluting him. It was a horrific scene that consumed my mind until we crossed the bridge and arrived at the hospital, with the staff standing outside the gate, waving and screaming loudly, "marhaba, marhaba", which is Arabic for "welcome". One of the women masterfully offered the traditional Arabic celebratory "zaghrota", the sound created by dancing the tongue in a rapid motion inside the mouth, a common happy gesture at weddings and festive occasions. Sure enough, it was truly a festive day, the first day of my first independent job.

The hospital building stood in the middle of a large lot facing the bridge and the canal, and surrounded by fields of maize and peanut, the two major crops of the region. After introducing themselves, the staff congregated in the central hall. Aliya, the older nurse, was dressed in a white gown and her head was covered by a white muslin scarf. She informed me in almost a motherly tone, that she also had functioned for years as the midwife of the region. An older man in his fifties, Mahdi, was the pharmacy technician and seemed to be the informal leader of the group. There were two other men, Hamza and Elwan, who provided support services and maintenance. The two younger women, Hosnia and Faukia, were nursing assistants. The hospital clerk and receptionist, Mansour, was a young man who was a somewhat more polished city man, who lived with his family in the town of Abu Hammad and commuted daily on his bike. Finally, there was Hamouda, who had recently joined the staff and had not yet been assigned a task. Apparently, at that time, following the final departure of the British troops, as negotiated by President Nasser in the summer of 1956 before the Suez Canal war erupted, there was significant unemployment in the region, as many of the inhabitants of the various nearby villages had been employed by the British troops, for support and maintenance services. As the local provincial government became concerned with the economic impact at the end of the British presence around the nearby Suez Canal, the government ordered many government facilities, such as schools and rural hospitals, to create more jobs, for the sake of employment rather than a real need of more manpower.

By the time the staff introductions had ended and the last round of traditional Egyptian black tea had been offered, it was almost noon and time for a private meeting with Mr. Saddiqui, a retired wealthy lawyer who had served in Cairo in a senior civil service position at the Ministry of Health. After his retirement and return to his native village of Bani Ayoub, he built a nice, modern villa that stood out among the dark, mud-brick primitive houses. Mr. Saddiqui served as the sage and benevolent patron of the Bani Ayoub region, donating his advice and the help of his political and government connections. I was told that he was instrumental in expediting the old plans to develop a rural hospital in Bani Ayoub. In reality, for me it was a bit too much to call the building a hospital, since it looked like a typical storefront dispensary or an expanded outpatient clinic, however, it was officially referred to as a hospital. Accompanied by Mahdi, the most senior pharmacy technician, whose job was dispensing the not so many available medications and preparing daily a number of colourful and popular potions according to an old version of the British Pharmacopoeia. Most popular among them, according to Mahdi, were the carminative "Rhubarb and Soda" and the crimson red tonic "Iron and Quinine", which all likely exploited and benefited from the magical power of the placebo. Walking along the very narrow and tortuous streets of the village, the beautiful and modern structure of Mr. Saddiqui's villa became visible among the dark modest houses around it. I recall my immediate perception of the villa as being an anomalous structure, not that it wasn't beautiful among the seemingly ugly, dark surroundings. Later on, reflecting more on my distorted perception, I could only think about the painful reality of coming face-to-face with the sad, but serious, inequality in the countryside, which was likely further distorted by my socialist leanings at that time.

Upon arrival, a tall and thin Mr. Saddiqui, looking his age of seventy years, was waiting for us on the front porch of the villa, where Mahdi waited for the welcoming lunch that followed. Mr. Saddiqui led me to a private meeting in his study room, which looked more like an old country lawyer's office, with the stacks of thick books and files overflowing the shelves. It was a most pleasant welcome by a very pleasant man, who reminded me of my father, with his polite gestures of kindness. He updated me with his concerns about the economy and general health of the population that was rapidly decreasing by the departure of the younger population to the cities, for study or work. After about half-an-hour, Mr. Saddiqui accompanied me to the front porch, where some thirty people of the region's notables were invited for a welcoming lunch. The guests were seated on cushions on the floor around a few large and round low tables (tablea) and only one regular table with a few chairs that stood in the middle of the porch, for myself and other officials of the region: the omda, the school principal and the postman, who were seated around it. After a welcome speech by the omda, lunch was served in the Bedouin village tradition; large urns of fata were served, which was freshly baked corn bread, soaked in a thick lamb broth, covered by a layer of steamed rice and topped with big chunks of boiled lamb.

Then it was time to return with Mahdi to the hospital, which served as my daytime home-base in the village for the next two years. Plans for the next day were discussed and the driver of the car taking me back to Abu Hammad alerted me to his presence, but the one and only thought that never left my mind that day was the mental picture of the emaciated, stuporous man I saw on my way to the hospital. I sort of knew what the problem could be, but I worried if I would be able to help the poor man and prevent a likely death, which would provide a bad omen for a young new medical doctor in his very early days of medical practice.

Face to Face with Endemic Pellagra and "Pellagra Madness"

The next day, my second day on the job, I arrived on time at about ten o'clock, with only one thought in mind; to make a home visit to the sick man I had noticed the day before on my way to the hospital. I declined the staff's suggestion to see him in the hospital, even if they had to carry him there. At noon, accompanied by two of the staff who happened to know the patient and his family well, we arrived at the house after a few minutes walk and were welcomed by several relatives, then led inside to a poorly lit room that had no doors or windows. There was the patient, lying down on a carpet on top of the large clay oven that extended from wall to wall, which was the traditional sleeping area in villages. The man was disoriented and did not recognize who we were or the purpose of our visit.

A detailed history from relatives revealed the man had been sick for almost two years. It started with feeling weak and unable to continue working in the fields. His face and the exposed parts of his limbs and body were reddish, which was blamed by the family as related to long exposure to the sun. But as the man got more progressively ill, he started vomiting and having long bouts of diarrhea. He visited the regional hospital in Abu Hammad, was admitted for a few days and then discharged as being a bit better. He was advised to take some medications, but after a couple of weeks he stopped taking them. He returned to farming for a while, but slowly and gradually became less attentive, frequently in a daze and disoriented. He stayed home and was unable to eat as a result of painful sores on his tongue and mouth, as well as a loss of appetite. He became emaciated, stuporous and apathetically silent most of the time. It was a typical history of advanced pellagra in a region that relied on maize as the main dietary staple. The medical and neurological examination was consistent with complications of pellagra. His liver was enlarged, his feet were swollen and edematous, his skin was covered with dark brown rough crusts and his tendon reflexes were impaired, and, mentally, he presented with a picture of pellagra-like dementia, being severely cognitively impaired. A classic picture and once you see it, it's hard to miss.

It was a most interesting coincidence, as the topic of pellagra was at the top of my mind during the last rotation in Medicine, at the end of my house officer years a few months earlier. At that time, I had volunteered to serve a month of my three months of medicine rotations in the chronic tuberculosis ward in the Kasr-al Aini Hospital, which a few other students had declined. It was a large ward that housed chronic patients of inactive tuberculosis, but suffered from severe chest complications. Their lungs were filled with cavities, they were desperately short of breath and many of them didn't survive long. It was almost a palliative care program, without the name attached to it.

The patients were treated with a mix of the newly discovered antibiotic streptomycin, and another medication called isoniazid. A most interesting observation at that time was that many patients developed reddish skin, their faces were distinctly pink and the skin became unhealthy and scaly, a picture that was described as "pellagra-like" complications, but without knowing its cause. Only later was the mystery uncovered when it was discovered that isoniazid was an antagonist of vitamin B6, an important nutritional ingredient of the family of vitamin B complex. Another curious and equally mysterious observation was that many of the patients on isoniazid appeared to be exceptionally cheerful, with a good mood that at times was labelled mildly hypomanic. A strange picture, on the face of their grim outcome. It took a few years to unravel the mystery, as isoniazid was discovered to have antidepressant properties by increasing the availability of certain brain chemicals that energized some brain receptors. Sure, it was a grim month of frequent fatalities, but the learning and medical experiences were invaluable.

Now, with an almost clear diagnosis of the sick man in Bani Ayoub, the challenge was what to do. The first and most relevant advice was to arrange an admission to the regional hospital in Abu Hammad, advice that the family vehemently turned down. In their uninformed mind, admission to the hospital meant that the man was near death and their preference was for him to die at home or, alternatively, he be treated at home and, hopefully, would get better. It was a serious challenge and a dilemma on my second day in Bani Ayoub, for a young physician at the beginning of a medical practice with no one available to consult. The one clear issue in my mind was not to force admission to the hospital, but to work with the family for a couple of weeks, pushing treatment and to wait and see. The family was more comfortable and cooperative with such an approach. After all, the man had been in such a pathetic state for a while. His condition, as I described in my notes, was in a state of "stable instability". So I assigned a nurse for his daily homecare, hydrated him enough and loaded him with extra doses of nicotinamide, which was the missing nutrient in his chronic diet. Loads of brewer's yeast was added, which was the cheapest and most readily available nutritional supplement. Plus, I used a good part of my small discretionary budget to help the family properly feed him, buying meat, vegetables and fruits, a practice that officially was not permitted, but I did not mind breaking the rules for such a serious medical situation.

The nurse visited daily and I saw the patient a few times a week. Progress was slow, but in two weeks the man became more animated, with signs of some life coming back. We persisted and in about three months a noticeable improvement was the talk of the village and the region; and instant fame and recognition for the young physician, that got out of proportion, acquiring mythical and, at times, mystical overtones, thanks principally to the cheap brewer's yeast that was already freely and routinely given to the residents. The village was almost as if awakened from lethargy, and the young men who frequented the clinic complaining of weakness, meaning sexual weakness without saying it, significantly dropped over the next few months, after distributing brewer's yeast tablets freely in the village. Truly a significant story in my budding interest in neurosciences. So, what is pellagra, the mysterious illness that brought me fame and shaped my career interests?

Pellagra: What Is It?

Pellagra is a nutritional deficiency disorder that was first described in the north of Spain and Italy. Initially, it was named "Mal de la Rosa" (the disease of the rose) as a result of the pinkish colour of the skin. Subsequently, it was known as the disease of rough skin (pelle agro), which over time the two words were fused into one: pellagra. The disease became well recognized for its particular skin lesions, which form thick, dark brown blotches and crusts on the face and exposed areas all over the body, similar to burnt toast. Usually, its onset was accompanied by severe gastrointestinal problems that began with painful ulcerations on the tongue and quickly spread to vomiting and diarrhea, resulting in severe dehydration. As the disease progresses, its impact on brain function leads to apathy, lethargy and cognitive impairment, producing a picture like dementia. It is interesting that in our class visit to the Abbassyia Mental Hospital in 1954, among the chronic residents of the old asylum were a number of cases of pellagra-related irreversible dementia. It was one of the five most common causes for admission to the old asylum, as we were told then. Nowadays it is much less frequent, compared to its wide-spread presence in the past, as seen in northern Italy, Spain, the southern US, Mexico, Egypt and several other African and South American countries. It was particularly common in countries that depended on the consumption of maize as the most common dietary staple, such as in the region of Bani Ayoub, with its sandy soil that allows for cultivation of only a few hardy crops. Initially, several theories were advanced about its cause, ranging from a toxic mould growing on corn cobs or a toxic substance in maize that was released during the process of digestion in the gut. By the 1900s, it became endemic in the southern US, which was related to nutritional protein deficiency, in general, but the attention specifically focused on certain amino acids such as tryptophan and others. It wasn't until 1937, when its specific cause was serendipitously discovered. It turned out that some dogs were known to develop a black swollen tongue that would resolve after feeding the dogs a diet that was rich in nicotinic acid and vitamin B complex. Trials with nicotinic acid in patients suffering from pellagra yielded good results almost magically. Subsequent research then identified specifically a nicotinamide deficiency as the cause of the disease, which became the standard treatment practice. That is why brewer's yeast, rich in nicotinamide and other vitamin B complex ingredients, proved significantly helpful among the Bani Ayoub population, since many of them were suffering from different grades and shades of nutritional deficiency. Nowadays, with the noticeable improvement in nutrition, generally, pellagra has become much less common, except in severe cases of malnutrition. As a medical student, I recall memorizing pellagra as the disease of three Ds: Dermatitis, Dementia and Death. But, not anymore.

Reflections on the Issue of Placebo Responses

In 1945, just a few years before I enrolled at Cairo University for my medical studies, a well known professor, O.H. Perry Pepper, a professor of medicine at the University of Pennsylvania and the president of the Pennsylvania College of Physicians, published in the American Journal of Pharmacy an intriguing paper with the title: "A Note on the Placebo", that in a few years became a must-read for medical students and young doctors. The well known professor opened his paper with a statement that read: "It's interesting that apparently there has never been a paper published discussing the important subject of the placebo". Professor Pepper cited the absence of this topic from the index of the US Surgeon General's library and from the Cumulative Medical Index. He added: "No doubt this valuable item of our therapeutic armament is mentioned repeatedly in articles under other headings, but it deserves at least one reference all its own". He went on to provide an interesting historical review of the word "placebo", which was described in various different terms. One of the definitions that stuck for some time, a placebo was considered as an "epithet" given to any medicine and adopted more to please than to benefit, which was rather contradictory in substance and mostly negative in tone.

At that time, physicians in the early era of medicine lacked the knowledge or the methods to distinguish drugs which had true actions from those that lacked any action. During the 19th and early 20th centuries, placebos used to be freely prescribed all over the world. Each famous physician chose a favourite name for his or her placebo. As Professor Pepper outlined in his 1945 paper, the important attributes of an effective placebo, in addition to the lack of any pharmacological action, its name had to be unknown to the patient and preferably given a Latin polysyllabic name and was to be given with assurance and emphasis for its therapeutic value. Not surprising, then, that some of the unusual placebo names used by some famous physicians included names such as "Tincture Confurango" or fluid-extract of "Cimicifuga Nigra", etc., which were nothing more than sugar pills. For the next twenty to thirty years, the topic of placebo garnered extensive scientific interest, generating volumes and volumes of publications, much more than the one dedicated paper that Professor Pepper wished for in his 1945 publication. Its popularity was further enhanced by the introduction of placebo-controlled clinical studies of new medications. With the thousands of research publications and the many extensive reviews, the question still due is whether we already know everything we need to know about placebos, their effects and their psycho-neurobiology. Unfortunately, my answer is "not yet". Basic issues, such as agreeing on an appropriate definition, continues to be unsettled. It is paradoxical to still define placebos as inert substances devoid of pharmacological actions, when several neuroimaging studies have already demonstrated clear actions on certain regions of the brain that are basically involved in the regulation of emotions, pleasure, pain and self-awareness. We already have extensive knowledge about the attributes of the placebo that can enhance its effects. Shape, size, colour, route of administration, the environment in which treatment takes place, as well as the strength of the therapeutic relationship between the doctor and the patient has all been documented to impact placebo response and strength. The search for specific attributes to describe the placebo responder's personality proved inconsistent, as it seemed like a search for a fictitious personality. Interesting that many of the issues thought to enhance placebo response has also been thought of later by us, and others, to be the same issues that have frequently been implicated in patients' satisfaction and achieving good outcomes. Several psychological processes have been proposed and investigated as the mechanisms belying the placebo response. Suggestion, persuasion, expectations and conditioning were among the issues explored, but without any clear agreement on how much each contribute. It stretches credulity a bit reading an old case report about the psychologist who committed suicide by ingesting a bottle of placebo.

Indeed, placebos do work and can elicit a measurable response, as already demonstrated in several medical conditions, including chronic pain, irritable bowel syndrome, anxiety, depression, etc. In clinical trials of new medications, having a high placebo response does not necessarily mean failure of the new drug, since the response to placebo or the drug could be related to different pharmacological mechanisms.

Why, then, are placebos not used in clinical practice? It is true that the placebo response provides the clearest indication of how close the link is between the mind and the body. The problem is that placebos, by definition, include a clear element of deception, which in most of the situations poses an ethical challenge. Any use of a placebo, whether in clinical trials of new medications or exceptional clinical situations, has to be grounded in a clear, ethical framework. Not doing so can create serious consequences, as has already happened, unfortunately, in a few clinical studies. I read one study published in 1971, in The American Journal of Obstetrics and Gynecology, which reported data from a placebo-controlled study of the contraceptive pill side effects. Not surprisingly, a number of unwanted pregnancies were reported in the placebo group. Even though, on the face of significant criticism, the authors defended the study design by reiterating that the women signed a consent form and were told about such a risk; I believe the criticism still stands. Just how much did the poor women in the state of New Mexico understood the terms of the consent form they had signed, particularly when the risk was irreversible? I believe that until we fully understand the mechanisms involved in the placebo response, we are not clear on the consistency of such a response and how long it lasts. Until that becomes clearer, a number of attributes to enhance placebo response, which have been consistently documented, can be employed to augment outcomes to therapy, without any fear of ethical infringement. Many of these attributes fall within what I later called "the extra-pharmacological" factors in treatment response, which include such issues as the strength of the patient/physician therapeutic relationship, and the social and environmental context in which the treatment takes place. The challenge, then, is to identify the components that contribute most and integrate them in clinical management. I do believe that the concept of placebo response needs to be revisited and reformulated as a positive force and an ally of medicine in improving therapeutic outcomes. I do believe that gaining more knowledge employing the recent brain neuroimaging technologies can hasten such a reformulated positive shift.

Bidding Farewell to Bani Ayoub - My Final Year as a Rural Physician

By the spring of 1959, almost a year after I arrived in Bani Ayoub, the popularity of the hospital, as noted by the significant increase of attendance from other far away regions, started to put a lot of strain on the staff and myself. The limited waiting space led to many patients having to wait a long time outside the building in the scorching sun. Neighbouring villages that were much bigger in size and population than Bani Ayoub, frequently expressed their frustrations and their continued grievances about the politics of choosing Bani Ayoub as the site for the hospital. A good solution suggested by the staff, that sounded reasonable and workable, was for me and a few of the staff to devote a few days every month travelling to a couple of nearby villages and seeing patients there. Soon the plan was in place and the logistics worked out. Finally, I had to travel by riding a donkey, which was not the easiest ride. Nevertheless, not only did the plan work in pacifying the discontent of other villages, but it also gave me the opportunity to become more familiar with the reality of the hard life in such a poor region. I visited many homes on medical visits and in response to several social invitations and other events. Most of the little houses everywhere were the typical mud brick structures, with a few houses here and there of more affluent residents, which were built with fired bricks and stones. Common to most of the houses I visited was the dual use of the house for both human inhabitants and their animals; cows, goats, chickens, etc., a very unsanitary and unhealthy mode of living. Every house generally accommodated two or three generations of the family.

On a medical home visit in the village of Bani Ayoub, 1959
(A sketch by the author, A.G. Awad, pen on paper 8" x 10")

At the same time, an amazing story was playing out in another old and well-established region, where villages were much more crowded than in Bani Ayoub, by the rapidly increasing populations. Some senior bureaucrats and politicians, who were unhappy about the explosive situation in many such villages, came up with a plan that appeared to be progressive and consistent with the government socialist agenda, building what was called the "model village", that were built in some remote areas on the edge of the desert. The houses were modern, with all the modern amenities and a separate space for animals in the backyard. The houses were to be given free to young families who, by choice, agreed to relocation. In addition, families were to be given a piece of land that needed to be prepared for cultivation. A bargain deal, but with nobody agreeing to relocate, which was a typical example of the well known fact of how much villagers in Egypt were completely tied and bound to their ancestral land at any cost. Finally, the government, after the embarrassment of the newly built, but deserted villages, resorted to pressure and began forcing some young families to relocate.

Sadly, in less than two years, a few of the model villages were deserted by the new inhabitants, who had fled in the dark of night to return to their crowded villages and escape being arrested by the guards who were placed there during the day. Such an embarrassing public "secret", which never was publicized by government agencies, touched me. It clearly demonstrated the faulty planning or the lack of planning. A better plan would have been to involve the young families in the crowded region to share and contribute to the planning process. It was a hard lesson and a costly missed opportunity. For me, such a big fiasco was attributed to a lack of information-sharing, that historically fuelled the resentment among villagers about their strong, but cynical, belief that nothing good can come from government at all levels, except for oppression and collecting more taxes.

The idea of having what I called "community get-togethers" in Bani Ayoub strengthened, as the staff and many residents of Bani Ayoub fully endorsed the idea. A monthly evening meeting was arranged, at the end of the day as the villagers were returning from the fields, and completely run by the residents and attended by some of the village officials; the omda or his delegate, the school principal and the Imam of the small mosque. And so the daily life and medical routine continued pleasantly, but with some intruding personal anxiety about my future career plans.

The good and, also, the bad news soon arrived by a formal letter from the National Commission for Studies Abroad about acceptance of my application, but instead of going to study in London, as I had planned, I was to be sent to Moscow. My subsequent protests did not lead anywhere, as the government insisted on their decision, or I was not going anywhere. The continued tense political and diplomatic situation between Egypt and the British government got much worse and continued after the Suez Canal War in 1956. The difficult economic crisis that followed the war deepened, creating a major concern about the government's hard currency funds. To make the situation much more complex, the government decreed that Egyptian physicians were not to be permitted to leave the country, except only with the permission of the Prime Minister's Office. The exodus of physicians to Saudi Arabia and the Emirates for better pay and working conditions took the government by surprise, though was clearly predicted. After a while, feeling like I'd not have another chance, particularly with the exceedingly tense political developments in Egypt and the clear and deep recognition of my status, being a member of the minority groups. I finally accepted, though I have to say that I agreed with some curiosity about what to expect in Moscow and behind the Iron Curtain. The date of going to Moscow was tentatively planned for January 1961. Meanwhile, there was a lot of back-and-forth discussion about the topic of my bursary in Moscow and why the government insisted to be within the field of neuro-endocrinology and experimental biology, a mystery that did not become clear for a few years, until my return to Cairo from Moscow in 1964, almost four years later.

I decided not to share the information with the staff until a couple of months later, to allow for further manoeuvring to try to change my destination, but with no luck. In the midst of all these evolving concerns, I received a formal letter from the Ministry of Health, in Cairo, informing me that the little "hospital" in Bani Ayoub had been chosen to develop a birth control clinic, as part of a program funded by an American development foundation, possibly the Rockefeller Foundation, that was heavily involved in funding major projects in the US and internationally, for the purpose of social engineering. After a busy sixty years, the memory gets a bit hazy about particular details, but, intuitively, I believe it was the Rockefeller Foundation. Though part of me had quickly welcomed the idea, soon after I started to worry about multitudes of issues, including my deep conviction that the sparsely populated region of Bani Ayoub did not need any birth control clinics. How could I get the religious staff motivated to make the project be successful, particularly for the concerns of the senior female nurse, Alyea, who practiced as a midwife for a couple of decades? To my surprise and comfort, her response as I shared the information was very measured and understanding, which made the other staff more comfortable with the idea, recognizing that no one had a choice.

Soon the logistics were resolved, the supplies arrived, including the newly developed contraceptive pill, with the confidential request not to widely publicize it and to encourage enrolment. The women were to be given money, ten piastres monthly, upon attending the clinic and taking the pills. The date was set for opening the clinic in mid-April. There were few more meetings in Cairo with Ministry of Health officials, who explained that the pill was already approved for use as a treatment for menstrual disorders and would be shortly approved as a contraceptive by the FDA (Food and Drug Administration). In one such meeting, I was asked to connect with a professor of obstetrics and gynecology, the late Professor Fouad Al-Hifnawi, who was the Ministry consultant and the future director of a planned academic unit at the National Egyptian Research Council, in Cairo;

the Unit of Reproductive Biology and Family Planning. Among all the other concerns and my mind full to capacity with thoughts, mostly unpleasant ones regarding Moscow, meeting Professor Al-Hifnawi proved to be the brightest and most enjoyable event at that time. He offered me the opportunity to help him in developing the new program until my departure for Moscow and, upon my return, I could join him, officially serving in an academic position in their recently developed National Research Institute.

Time passed quickly, as the clinic turned out to be a great success, without any big fanfare except by word of mouth. Most likely, the quick success was related more to the ten piasters incentive, which was not a small amount at that time for the average poor village residents. Though there was debate between myself and the staff of whether we needed the consent of the women's husbands or not, the issue continued to be unresolved without any clear guidance from the Ministry of Health. My monthly meeting with Professor Al-Hifnawi continued, with the near realization that finally my ambition to become an academician and researcher in reproductive biology was getting closer. I was asked to prepare a review documenting the alarming population growth in Egypt, which completely took my mind off the concerns about my future life in the Soviet Union.

The date of my departure to Moscow was settled for January 23, 1961, which would introduce me for the first time to the frozen Moscow winter. I got busy looking for the heaviest coat I could find in Egypt, for survival in Moscow's winter. But then an unplanned event dented the rising and acclaimed success of the birth control clinic in Bani Ayoub, an observation by the staff that some small fish in the canal facing the hospital were floating dead downstream. Some quick detective observations by the staff revealed that after leaving the clinic, some of the women holding the pills and the ten piastres, dropped the pills from over the bridge into the slow-moving water in the little canal. Once more, a great idea almost ended in failure, like the experiment of the "model village". By the time the situation was discussed and re-reviewed a few times, some measures were implemented, including the provision of more public information to the population, in defiance of the Ministry of Health edicts.

As all that got sorted out, my time for departure in January 1961 approached. I said goodbye to the staff and many of the inhabitants of Bani Ayoub, whom I had gotten to know and share with them my empathy and frequently sad feelings about their difficult and impoverished life. I spent a few days with my family in Zagazig before I left for Cairo and my trip to the unknown, with feelings of gratification for the valuable experiences I had in Bani Ayoub, but also with some sadness about tasks not yet fully accomplished.

PART III

My Moscow Years (1961-1964)

Departing to Moscow – The Flight to the Unknown

Awaiting my flight to Moscow, with one overnight stop in Copenhagen on January 23, 1961, I finally had the chance to meet the other three companions who, like me, were travelling to Moscow for post graduate studies. Two of them were engineers from Cairo University and the third was a biologist. We flew with "Misr Air", which was the official carrier for those travelling on government business. The flight was enjoyable and comfortable, with everyone's mind likely, as with myself, occupied by the thoughts of what life would be like in Moscow.

On arrival to Copenhagen for a much welcomed one night stop-over before a flight the next day to Moscow, we were booked into a very nice hotel named Hotel Axelborg. It was right in the centre of the city, facing the famous Danish amusement park Tivoli Gardens, where we managed to squeeze in a short visit the next morning. My major and urgent concern was to go shopping quickly for a more appropriate heavy coat and warm hat, as I realized that my Cairo coat proved inadequate, even for the much milder winter climate in Copenhagen. By early that evening, we were back to the Copenhagen airport for our flight to Moscow. Noticeably, all of us were in a somewhat somber mood, even after having a very enjoyable time in Copenhagen.

Upon arrival to the Moscow Airport, it was already late evening and dark. We were met by an official from the Soviet Ministry of Universities and High Education, who surprised us by introducing himself in Arabic as "Abu Hassan". He did not look like an Arab or Middle Eastern, and it turned out that he was originally from Belarus (a White Russian Soviet state) and had studied the Arabic language in one of the Soviet middle Asian states. He spoke in a mostly literary version and not in the street colloquial dialect that is generally used in Egypt. I recall how he sounded a bit funny, like a caricature. That reminded me of lectures given in Cairo by some foreign visiting professors in their attempts to speak in Arabic, who were referred to as the "Orientalists" by the well known cultural and social critic Professor Edward Said, in his book "Orientalism". We received special treatment, being processed for entry in a special VIP section. The immigration officers, though polite, looked stern and emotionless and it felt almost as if we were being processed before entering a jail. Their English was minimal, but certainly much better than our knowledge of the Russian language. A couple of hours later, Abu Hassan drove us to a student hostel for the night, before taking us next day to our respective student hostels, that were dependent on the institute that we individually would join.

I felt too tired to get angry and upset about the poor living conditions of our first night in Moscow. Bathroom amenities lacked warm water, toilet paper and even a toilet seat. The dining cafeteria was already closed for the night, but we were given a few boiled sausages, some cooked cabbage and a piece of dark bread, an unappetizing meal that no one touched. The next morning, after a similar breakfast, I was driven to the student hostel where medical graduate students were housed. Living conditions there appeared to be not much better, but I was given a rather comfortable room, shared with a Russian graduate student who was studying physical medicine and spoke very little English. Pairing a foreign student with a Russian student was by design, according to the rules, to enhance the quick acquirement of the Russian language by foreign students through our somewhat limited conversations. It sounded reasonable, but was a bit frustrating initially, and later on I learned that such pairing of room occupancy also had another motive of keeping a close eye on foreign students and regularly reporting on them to the authorities.

In a couple of days, I joined a prearranged tour to visit Moscow's Red Square and its beautiful ancient churches and buildings that represented the centre of power. However, walking around in the twenty-four-degrees-below-zero temperature, even with the Copenhagen coat and hat, proved to be an impossible task. Assurances that the winter of 1961 was considered a mild winter not only failed to help, but was alarming, considering that I had four winters to survive. In a few days I started to feel frustrated, I could not go out for walks and the student hostel was crowded and noisy. My room was close to the main kitchen on that floor, which meant an endless crowd of Chinese, Vietnamese and East Asians who congregated in the kitchen to prepare their own meals in their own cuisine, which was not familiar to me and I was troubled by its repugnant smells at times.

The plan for me was to start courses for the study of the Russian language before the beginning of my medical studies in July, at the assigned Institute of Experimental Endocrinology. My discontent and complaints with my living situation mounted, as well as those of the other foreign students. Persuaded by advice from a foreign student who had been in Moscow for a couple of years, who told me that if you do not vigorously complain in the Soviet Union you will never get a resolution, I did just that. In a few days, I was told that the plan had changed and I would go to the University of Kiev for Russian language studies in the much warmer city of Kiev in the Ukraine, another state of the Soviet Union, located more southwest of Moscow. Another unplanned destination, but a welcome reprieve from the Moscow freeze.

Unplanned Detour to Kiev -A Surprise Destiny

A prearranged overnight one-thousand-kilometre train trip took me to Kiev, arriving in the morning of the next day. An English-speaking official welcomed me and drove me to the student hostel, where I would stay until June 1961. The weather was noticeably warmer, in a relative sense, only ten-degrees-below-zero! The reception was friendly and warmer than in Moscow. The general conditions of living were noticeably better and the big surprise was that I was given a room by myself for the first month, until a roommate would join me, a welcome gesture that elevated my spirits.

In a couple of days, I was given directions to meet with my Russian language teachers in the main building at the University of Kiev, which was a good twenty minutes of walking along a busy, but very nice street. I am sure that the weather was cold, but it seemed to be tolerable and enjoyable, and likely the different psychology in Kiev made it more manageable. It was hard to miss the Kiev University campus, as all the buildings were painted in clear red that made them stand out among other nearby buildings. The meeting with the head of the department of Russian Language Teaching for Foreigners, Maria F.P. and another senior teacher, Alexandra K., was pleasant and respectful. They communicated with me using their limited knowledge of English and I responded with my few Russian phrases that I had acquired during the couple of weeks in Moscow. The program was set for me to join a new class that would start about ten days later. At the end of the meeting, as a welcoming gesture, I was given a free ticket for a concert taking place a few days later at the Sports Palace.

Life started to gradually settle down, as it usually does following a period of emotional tensions. In a couple of days, the concert time was quickly due. I was provided with directions of how to reach the Sports Palace by bus, except that once I was on the bus, I quickly realized how difficult it was to follow the driver's stop announcements in Russian. After about twenty minutes of feeling lost, I stood up in the back of the bus and shouted in English, asking if anyone on the bus could speak English to let me know which was the stop for the Sports Palace. In a couple of minutes, a young woman stood up and in clear English she indicated that she also was going there. Problem solved, and not only was I to accompany her, but to my surprise and relief she volunteered to exchange her seat, so that she could sit beside me and explain the concert. It was like a sudden life-line had been extended to me, having an animated, though mostly formal, social conversation for the first time since I arrived in Moscow a few weeks earlier. At the end of the concert I profusely thanked her, we exchanged addresses and she left her phone contact in case I needed help. She accompanied me in the bus on our way back. My stop came earlier than hers and I disembarked, feeling a bit overwhelmed by the pleasant surprise.

In a few days, my Russian language class started with another six foreign students attending, mostly from African countries, but the surprise was that another Egyptian doctor was among the group and had just recently arrived from Cairo. It turned out that he was a lecturer in the department of Anatomy at Cairo University. He appeared pleasant, but quiet and rather kept to himself. He also was a practicing Coptic Christian and, like myself, he was rerouted to Moscow for post-graduate studies, which made me frequently wonder what an anatomist could study further in the Soviet Union. In a couple of weeks he asked to speak with me in private, which we did immediately, as he seemed to be somewhat distressed. It became clear that he was unhappy and seriously troubled about the weather and the state of accommodations, though he framed his concerns in a religious context about the value of any studies in a formally declared atheist society. We met a few times more and I suggested that he should speak about changing accommodations with the Russian officials who dealt with foreign students. I recommended that he request being moved to the hostel where I lived, knowing that they had available space. All of my arguments about us being sent to study science, not religion, was of little help to him. Even reminding him, as a Coptic Christian himself, about the situation of the radical religious groups we left behind in Egypt, who openly advocated for getting rid of religious minorities. In other words, no religion could be at times better than hostile and discriminative religious monopolies. Finally, in exasperation, I reminded him of the ancient historical facts about how the Catholic Church in medieval times forbade Christians from practicing anatomical dissection on human cadavers, which prevented Christians from becoming physicians and, according to the misguided religious interpretation that looking inside the human body had been the privy of only God, a decision that could have killed the science of anatomy and undermined all medical progress. All arguments appeared to be in vain, as he became entrenched and almost obsessed by his negative thoughts. In the end, he decided to go back to Egypt, which left me feeling sad and contemplating the issues of science and religion as a new intellectual interest of mine.

Meanwhile, my language studies were going well, thanks to the pedagogical expertise of my teachers and their fantastical human and highly cultured attitudes towards us. In less than six or seven weeks, I was able to find my way around using my newly acquired early skills in the Russian language. Yet, the most agonizing question in my mind was the deep wish to contact the young Russian woman who was so kind and helped me on my way to the concert, knowing, as I had been told by the Egyptian authorities, that contact with Soviet citizens outside the sphere of my studies was frequently monitored with suspicion and may have consequences. I hesitated and hesitated more, but in the end I decided to break the oppressive Soviet rule of talking to another human being who afforded me kindness when I needed it. It was a moment in life that proved eventually to be a flash of fate, rather than a rash personal decision. I did eventually phone her and, as frequently said, the rest is history. Our friendship steadily grew, with the clear understanding of the political sensitivity of the situation. She was a professional engineer in a rather sensitive job.

Her father, who had died a few years earlier, was a decorated war hero and a military engineer. Her mother came from a long line of Jewish ancestry, which made my friend Jewish, according to Jewish rules. As I sadly learned later, though her family was well respected and her father's contribution was recognized, the Jewishness of her mother, though nonpracticing, appeared at times to be a barrier in certain situations. Here I was, an Egyptian from a country that officially was at war with Israel, befriending a Soviet citizen who held a sensitive job and had shades of Judaism in the background; all the ingredients for us to get into trouble.

Yet, in the short time I spent in Kiev, our friendship got much closer and more personal. I was introduced and welcomed to a wide circle of her friends, that included several professionals and intellectuals, who were lamenting the Soviet system and yearning for a more liberal and decent democratic environment. It was a great learning experience for me, getting to know the hidden side of Soviet life. It presented a stark reality contrast of the majority of Soviet citizens blindly treated as a minority, compared to the privileged few who were party members. Such an oppressive social structure rekindled my submerged feelings about religious missuses and abuses, whether in Egypt or many other countries.

As the month of June approached, I completed my language studies, becoming able to read and write and to manage a reasonable conversation in Russian. The friendship that had grown with my two teachers carried me through the next three years in Moscow and extended for several years after my return to Cairo and, ultimately, until their death. The gift that I received upon completion of my language studies was a six-volume collection of poems and literary contributions by the celebrated and well-known Russian poet and writer Alexander Pushkin, and still to this day stands out prominently among my collection of ancient books, having survived the many translocations during the years that followed my Russian "expedition".

Much sadder were the feelings of leaving behind a trusted and valued friend, who three years later became my partner in life to this day. I am including this episode of my life in this story, which seems very personal in a book about psychiatry and neurosciences, because it shaped my becoming a fully engaged social human being. It defined forever the value of human relationships and its impact on my emotional maturity. Once more, such a pleasant turn of events underscored what I had already frequently encountered in my life; chance and unplanned events can sometimes turn out much better than planned ones. Not that one needs to ignore planning, but at the same time one has to be open to opportunities as suddenly as they may arise. With such pleasant contemplation, I left for Moscow.

My First Visit to the Institute of Experimental Endocrinology in Moscow

A few days after my return to Moscow, a meeting was set up with my supervisor at the All Union Institute of Experimental Endocrinology. I arrived on time early in the morning and was ushered into the office of Professor Youssef Abramovitch Eskin, who would be my PhD supervisor and was also the Director of the Experimental Biology Department. I was rather a bit worried about how my newly acquired Russian language would help me to explore the tens of questions I had in mind. The professor was in his early sixties, gentle and kind in his warm welcome. Jokingly, he smiled and informed me he had been waiting a long time for another man to join his large department of forty-two female scientists. He gave me a brief history of the Institute and the relatively new building that housed the research institute and a large hospital that specialized in the clinical management and research of endocrine disorders.

As I stumbled here and there to find the right Russian words, he quickly helped me, speaking in good English. It turned out that he spoke several languages; English, German, French and Yiddish, in addition to Russian and Ukrainian. He uncritically related his difficulties with the Egyptian authorities about the choice and scope of my thesis research topic. It turned out that the Egyptian authorities insisted on the focus of the research to include training in hormone bioassays, a topic that he strongly felt would become an obsolete field in a few years, considering the rapid technological advances in immunochemistry and the search for better methodologies. In his soft and fatherly voice he commented that in such conflicting situations with authorities, based on his experiences, he opted not to shut the door and say no to them, but to negotiate a solution that offered some compromise, to prevent the Egyptian government from cancelling the bursary and denying me the opportunity of post-graduate studies. It took until four years later, on my return to Cairo, to get to know the reason for the Egyptian government's insistence on my having bioassay experience, as will be described later. The compromise was then to include in my projects some training about the bioassay of the adrenal cortisol and other steroids produced by the cortex of the adrenal gland, while the main experimental topic would be about stress and the hypothalamic pituitary adrenal-axis response. I was happy to hear his suggestion, as the concept of stress and the major contributions of Professor Hans Selye, at McGill University in Montreal, was one of the most exciting scientific concepts of that time. It was also high on my list of choices for a research topic. I immediately agreed, as we discussed the logistics and the date for me to start my studies in the first week of July. I was provided with a few reprints of the professor's extensive publications, some historical information about the institute itself, which was rather young, having been founded in 1925, and other information about the discipline of endocrinology and its development in Russia and later on in the Soviet Union era. Another meeting was set up in a few days for me to be introduced to the senior scientists and the facilities of the institute, including a meeting with the seemingly powerful director, Professor Ekaterina Vosyoukova.

A couple of days later, I was back at the institute and warmly welcomed by the senior scientists, all of whom were women and a few were as old as Professor Eskin, but many were young. A quick tour included my little future office, which was not far from my boss's office and close to the laboratory where I would conduct my studies. We visited where the study animals were housed in a separate building, which included mice, rats of all types, guinea pigs, rabbits and even baboons. The meeting afterwards with Professor Eskin was a bit more personal than the first formal one, discussing the medical system, my Coptic background and then delving into ancient medicine and ancient Egyptian history. At noon my boss accompanied me for a short visit with the Director of the Institute, Professor Ekathrina Vasyoukova, who was in her sixties, pleasant and radiating an air of authority, giving me a brief synopsis of how the Institute was created in 1925 and how it became the premier institute for the clinical and research fields of endocrinology. She also shared information about the Institute's future plans to join the National Academy of Medical Sciences. She encouraged me that during my hospital clinical training period to take a close look and participate in the ongoing clinical trials for obesity in the context of diabetes, testing a new hypophysial extract from an ox's brain. I left encouraged and more satisfied about the inclusion of some clinical training in clinical trials, in addition to the experimental component.

Goats Milk and the Moscow All Union State Institute of Experimental Endocrinology

Though the discipline of endocrinology likely existed in many countries, including Russia, Britain, Germany, USA and other countries in the early nineteenth century, the institutions that focused on the clinical and research aspects of the rather young discipline varied in its development from country to country, according to the political and economic local circumstances. In Russia it was not until 1925, during the first decade of the Bolshevik revolution, that the Institute of Experimental Endocrinology was created as the first in Russia. The common tradition in Russia and all of Europe for using "organotherapy" (animal tissues extract) was well developed and used extensively. By 1924, when the Congress of the Russian Society of Endocrinology and many endocrinologists had convened in Moscow, there were enough endocrinologists researching organotherapy to press for the need for the development of an institute for endocrinology and hormonal organotherapy. The move was spearheaded by several well-known endocrinologists, including Iakov Tobolkin, who introduced and extensively published his research about thyroid hormones obtained from goats' milk extracts. Looking back on that era, it is interesting that the public environment at that time was fascinated and saturated by the publication of numerous science fiction stories about growing tissue or organs into full-grown human monsters. It also helped that the Bolshevik leaders, in their very early years, propagated the lofty notion that humanity could achieve immortality through their socialist communist propaganda programs.

Since its establishment in 1925, the Institute of Experimental Endocrinology focused on diabetes, thyroid and adrenal conditions as their major clinical interests. Their extensive research interests focused on the role of the hypothalamus, pituitary/adrenal axis and the impact of hormones on metabolic processes and obesity. In essence, then, my projected research plan experimentally exploring the impact of stress on the hypothalamic pituitary adrenal cortex was within their areas of expertise and interest.

Stress! - What is Stress?

The concept of stress is one of such a vague and nebulous state that, generally, it's much easier felt than defined or described. No wonder, then, of the various definitions that have been introduced over time. Frequently it has been defined by its impact or attributed to a specific condition, such as "post traumatic stress disorder" (PTSD), with its frequent diagnosis these days rivalling that of the flu. In my mind, the best description of stress was articulated by Hans Selye, the father of the modern concept of "general adaptation syndrome" (GAS), in 1936. This stress model was based on physiological and psychobiological responses to events that threaten an organism's state of well-being. He described the three stages of how the body responds to such a threat: Alarm first leads to resistance and then in adaptation, after long-term exposure. In other words, he popularized the concept of "fight or flight" that entered the popular lexicon, in terms of use of the phrase in any threatening situation. The concept of fight or flight had been described much earlier by the work of the psychologist Walter Cannon, working at Harvard University. In 1932, he described the fight or flight response occurring when a person experiences strong emotions, particularly due to something of a threatening nature.

Hans Selye, a medical doctor of Hungarian origin who studied medicine in Prague, travelled to New York on an American fellowship scholarship, but while on his return, he stopped in Montreal where he was offered a research job in 1930, in the Biochemistry Department at McGill University. Though his initial studies focused on sexual and reproductive aspects of lab animals, his focus shifted attention when he made the important observation that prolonged exposure to negative stimuli, such as surgical injury, severe cold or excessive exercise, the rats showed clear signs of adrenal gland enlargement and noticeable shrinkage of their thymus gland, as well the development of ulcers in their stomachs. His keen and intuitive observation led him to believe that such responses were not by chance, but triggered and coordinated by a process that led to such physiological responses. In reality, what Selye discovered was the original general adaptation concept. Its use of the word "stress" was borrowed from the physics of steel and how steel responds by reacting to a force. That was the beginning of the transformational concept of stress, and what was to follow for the next many years. The following identification of chemicals; cortisol and adrenaline, were the two chemicals behind the stress response. Such a discovery shifted the research focus to the hypothalamus-pituitary adrenal axis at the base of the brain, which became the research topic internationally of every second or third doctoral dissertation, no exaggeration, including mine in 1961.

Thus, Selye's concepts were broadly accepted as a major breakthrough. Several refinements and modifications followed, as well as a number of important critical concerns that were directed at his "biomedical" approach, related to the concepts of health and disease. One of the major criticisms was that biochemical changes did not necessarily translate to a disease entity. A disease is the ultimate outcome of the interaction of multiple factors at the cell molecular level, and a host of other social and environmental issues can exert a serious impact on the disease process. As already demonstrated later, the response to biological treatments can be influenced by psychosocial factors, as clearly noted by the powerful response to placebos. Adopting a clearly sick role is not necessarily associated with biological changes. The importance and the quality of the clinician-patient relationship cannot be overemphasized. These were a few of the critical comments of the Selye biomedical model of stress, many of which awaited for later research, including mine in Canada, that explored and clarified a number of issues in question. Yet, without any doubt, Selye's concepts proved to be of tremendous value in paving the way for our considerations about the state of health and disease.

One of the positive off shoots or extensions of Sely's adaption model was introduced a few years later, in 1977, by the social psychologist George Engel, under the title of "Biopsychosocial Model". His purpose was to introduce a more holistic alternative to the biomedical model that seemed to separate the mind and the body. He recognized the importance of social, psychological and biological issues and their dynamic interaction related to illness and health. Engel's concept gained wide popularity and seemed to overcome the reductionist approaches and allowed for an important dialogue that included the patients and their families. In spite of some of the usual methodological criticism, the concept proved of immense clinical and practical value. The version that eventually evolved and became recognized as the "Vulnerability Stress Protection Model" gained wide applicability to the clinical and practical management of any illness. Its importance and beauty lies in its open structure that permitted the inclusion of any new factor revealed by new research. Additionally, vulnerability as a concept was not limited to innate factors such as genetics, but could also be externally created to include noxious environments or debilitating states in prolonged alcohol use, etc. The model is easy to grasp by patients and creates a useful dialogue, inviting the patient as a participant in the process of their own recovery. It allows for realistic goals to enhance the many protective factors such as diet, exercise, meditation and healthy living to be considered. By far, among all the various proposed hybrid models. I believe that the vulnerability/stress/protection model, based on George Engel's early concepts, has proved to be the most useful and practical model in disease management. It is much more useful than the various explanations of mental illness that, unfortunately, are frequently used by psychiatrists, such as chemical imbalance or many other ill-informed explanations. Indeed, I have to point out that George Engel's concept had served as the conceptual inspiration for my later research contributions about wellness, quality of life, patient-centred care and a broad host of issues that I called the "extra-pharmacological" factors in drug response.

Sharing My Life in the Lab with Rats and Guinea Pigs

By early July 1961, I started my animal experiments on rats, with a noticeable enthusiasm that was augmented by the support I got from my supervisor and colleagues. It did not take a long time before encountering the complexity of animal research on the topic of stress.

The mere handling of the animal proved stressful enough to induce non-specific hormonal responses that complicated the interpretation of the experimental situation or medication. I had to find an animal model that would allow me not to handle the experimental animal or, at least, minimize it as much as possible. As is frequently said, necessity creates creativity. I had to develop a new model by which, under anaesthesia, two rats were surgically joined connecting the circulatory system in both, with one of the rats having the adrenal gland removed. In essence, creating conjoined twins. A complex and somewhat crude and cruel procedure that carried a high rate of fatality among the operated rats, but after a period of recovery and adaptation the surviving pairs allowed the manipulation of the hypothalamo-hypophyseal and adrenal system without touching the rat with the intact adrenal gland. Looking back on what appears now to be primitive and cruel experimentation, one is astounded by how much medical technology and knowledge has advanced. A few years after completing my studies, biological hormone assays were abandoned all together in favour of the new methodology of radioimmunoassay. I do strongly believe that without the development of such modern immunoassay, the field of neuroendocrinology would have never progressed and could have died. In essence, without the continual development of modern new medical technologies, no further progress would be expected in any discipline of medical sciences, including psychiatry and the neurosciences. Looking back on that period of time in conducting my experimental studies, I really was distressed at times with the complexity of the methodology. In spite of the great technical support and help from colleagues, there were a few moments that I regretted my choice of such a complex topic. However, that was where determination and some innate resilience kept me going and looking forward to my clinical training in the hospital. As my clinical assignment was initially in the thyroid program, but then moved to the diabetes and obesity unit, it was a valuable opportunity to observe human behaviour and the way some patients wilfully defeated the reason for which they were hospitalized and had been enrolled in a serious and controlled clinical study for the treatment of obesity. The medications that were under investigation were named interestingly as "Adiposin", which was a tissue extract of the hypophysial region of ox brains. A strict protocol was observed, with no visitors nor food from outside being allowed during the first four weeks of the trial. A number of patients lost some weight, but another group of patients, on the contrary, appeared to gain weight. Enhancing the exercise program and closely observing the number of consumed calories did not reveal the reason, until one evening when a patient was caught lowering down from a third-floor window a long rope attached to a small basket which carried up forbidden food items. It was a very interesting experience altogether, that clearly confirmed my passion for clinical work with human beings and not with rats or guinea pigs, which I have never touched since then.

The Life of a Foreign Graduate Student in the Moscow of the Early 1960s

I have to admit that in spite of the many complaints about communal life in the Moscow student hostels, generally, foreign students were accorded more privileges than the average non-party Russian students. I was fortunate to reside most of my years in Moscow in one of the better accommodations, situated at a central location in the city. From my room window on the fourth floor of a large soviet-style building, I could see the nearby grand skyscraper of the 1950s Soviet architecture of the late Stalinist era, located on the well-known Smolinski Boulevard and still hosts the mega Ministry of Foreign Affairs.

My room was rather austere, but comfortable by Soviet standards and expectations. Nearby, there was a large kitchen that served as the centre of action and noise on that floor. It was frequented by the many Chinese and South Asian students; Vietnamese, Korean and others, to prepare their meals according to their preferred national cuisines, using some of the exotic food items unfamiliar to me and that created at times unpleasant food aromas. But, generally, the environment was basically friendly, with every national group sticking mostly to themselves and conversing in their own language. On Friday evenings and Saturdays, the floor became much more alive and noisy, as parties and friends were allowed to visit, with lots of drinking, cooking and loud music. On special occasions the celebration could get wild, as in celebrating Soviet space accomplishments or political events. During weekdays the floor used to be empty and quiet, with most students having gone to pursue their studies. For me, a student day began early in the morning, but my end of the day entirely depended on my lab experiments and frequently resulted in staying extra hours.

In some way, life in a student hostel presented itself as a microcosm representing life in the outside world. At that, the City of Moscow was filled by all kinds of different nationalities from the other Soviet states within the Soviet Union or from the Soviet block countries, particularly from Hungary, Romania and Czechoslovakia, but also many from Africa, Cuba and Latin America, representing the era of the Soviet diplomatic expansion all over the world.

After a while, living in the large student hostel, making some acquaintances, chatting here and there or invited to some Saturday parties, one could recognize the two worlds that existed in the building; the routine daily active world, but also another underground world, mostly secretive and not open to everyone except for those well trusted. Students who were active in the communist parties had their network that frequently served as the political link with higher party organizations on the outside. They also served another layer of secret monitoring, particularly of foreign students who, by and large, were mostly aware of being monitored. It was interesting that I was advised on our arrival to Moscow by an official in the Egyptian embassy to be extra careful, as foreigners were closely followed and watched. I laughed as I wondered how the Russian authorities would be able to follow the thousands of foreigners in Moscow, an advice that I decided not to let limit my freedom to conduct my life appropriately, as I did everywhere. As I became aware of the underground political network in the student hostel and probably everywhere else people lived together, I realized that the secretive control of individuals was accomplished from within, by fear and caution of being watched that was deeply instilled, a clever ploy but a wicked way of control and suppression. Anyway, I conducted my life unfazed by the many threatening stories that were easily propagated by the authorities themselves. I admit that I had no conflicts or incidents and was treated respectfully everywhere, and also I behaved in a respectful way.

Another significant underground grouping was well-known as "samizdat", which was the network of hand-written distribution of prohibited books, mostly with anti-Soviet themes, including political documents and opinion pieces. In my first year in Moscow, several underground reports about the 1956 communist party central political committee were circulating. Apparently, in that extraordinary and highly political meeting serious decisions were made to change the soviet political course by purging the oppressive Stalinist era and charting a new course. That was then still the hottest item circulating underground. With the death of the writer Boris Pasternak in 1960, and the prohibition of his novel, "Dr. Zhivago", a Russian copy was smuggled, printed and circulated by the CIA in Amsterdam during the international world's fair, and found its way to the samizdat network, until it finally got officially published later. Similarly, by the time the prohibited novel by the writer Aleksander Solzhnetsyn, "One Day in the Life of Ivan Denisovitch", was making the run underground until it eventually got official approval from Khrushchev to be printed in the magazine "Novi Mir" (The New World). It was fascinating, but also frightening, the degree of strict control of freedom of speech or anything that got close to the slightest political criticism. I frequently had the strange feeling that many such secret documents were leaked by government party members to the underground samezdat, to serve other ulterior motives.

As I used to take a vacation in the summer to visit my family in Egypt or travel to Europe, I usually was given a list of desired gifts requested by friends and colleagues in Moscow, such as bottles of scotch whisky, nylon women's stockings or toiletry. The one item I refused to oblige was bringing in books, which were treated as terrorist items. Otherwise, there were several aspects of enjoyment such as easy access to the most hard to get tickets for performances at the Bolshoi Theatre or the Taganka drama theatre. Show tickets very quickly began to serve as a useful currency in bartering or facilitating life issues. Though, as foreigners we were not allowed to leave the city or go anywhere beyond thirty kilometres from the city centre, I frequently managed to do it and even at times travelling by train for over a thousand kilometres to Kiev, for a visit to my girlfriend and my Russian language teachers or sneaking to the Crimea, visiting the city of Yalta on the Black Sea.

Once or twice a year I would spend a good part of a day in the town of Zagorsk, which was about seventy kilometres from Moscow, and had been renamed Sergeyev Posad. It used to be my spiritual retreat, with its architecturally unique churches and monastery that were founded in the fourteenth century by Saint Sergius of Radonezh. Through the centuries of wars, fire and neglect, the monastery survived and is still functioning as the centre of the Russian Orthodox Church. It also served as the centre of iconoclastic art, including its many historical icons by famous artists, such as the Trinity Icon by the famous painter Andrea Rublev. In 1961, the authorities began a long-term restoration, which, unfortunately, limited access to many of the historic churches. Yet, just being there among the many religious historical relics would put oneself face to face with the long Russian history of resistance and suffering that defined the soul of Russian life. In essence, the life of a foreign graduate student, such as my life in Moscow, was a great mix of personal experiences surrounded by its rich history and arts, but lacking the feeling of being free. Day to day life was sometimes rather difficult, as it got complicated by fleeting feelings of loneliness and being away from one's original environment in Cairo, as much as one may have disliked it or detested it there.

By the spring of 1964, my experimental studies were almost completed and, as in life, there is always a beginning and then there is the end that was slowly approaching. It was a time to step back and take a look at what had been accomplished. My life had fortunately been quite settled, as I felt almost fully integrated into the life of the department, aided and at times pampered by the extra attention from all the bright and hardworking women scientists around me. I had managed to accumulate lots of data and experimental observation that required a good deal of sifting to separate the wheat from the chaff, and this turned out to be the most challenging part. To create a good coherent thesis that can be presented and defended proved to be not easy and required a good deal of creative guessing to make the story about the future, rather than reporting the status quo. That was where I needed the help that I got from my supervisor and colleagues. Light was obvious at the end of the tunnel, but the challenge was now to master the difficult journey of navigating the tunnel in my goal to successfully defend my thesis and achieve my PhD.

Looming in the background was the immanent notion that once I completed my task, I had to leave. But, before leaving I needed to settle the more difficult personal matter of getting married, which required official permission from the Egyptian embassy. Obtaining a formal permission was not the greatest obstacle, which turned out to be the delicate and emotional details of my future wife being an only child. Luckily, all concerns one way or another were resolved in a short time. Marriage in the Russian Soviet tradition was simple and very touching. An application for an appointment at the Wedding Palace in Moscow was accepted, and a date and time were booked. An hour was allocated and the many ceremonies that were booked that day took place on the hour, like a conveyor belt. The ceremonies were conducted in a beautiful palace, with music, a judge presiding and the attendance of only a few friends, all for a just nominal fee. Since that moment, such a simple and inexpensive marriage ceremony established itself in my mind as the smartest and most practical wedding procedure that I frequently recommended to relations and friends, but, sadly, my advice was never taken by anyone else.

The defence of my thesis in front of a national panel of scientists was not simple, but with the many questions, queries and clarifications, it ended successfully, at least, that's how I felt. It was a great relief worth a celebration, but now I had to leave, as my Russian visa would expire shortly and my Russian "expedition", as I used to call it, was coming to an end.

Living in an Atheist Society - Reflections on Science and Religion

By the time I arrived in Moscow in 1961, the Soviet Union as a country had been formally declared an atheist society since the 1917 Bolshevik take-over of power. It was not just the absence of religions, it was in reality a declared and systematic fight against religion. The official stance on religion was what was called "scientific atheism". Religions were banned, churches demolished or converted for other uses and the clergy, mostly from the Russian Orthodox church, were jailed or exiled. Religious teachings in schools were abandoned and replaced by Marxist Leninist teachings. Such a repressive and coercive banning of everything religious got a brief reprieve by Stalin during the Second World War, to encourage and invite national public support for the war efforts. Unfortunately, by the end of the war, such a brief tolerance disappeared. Following the death of Stalin in 1954, the repressive attitude against religions seemed to soften a bit, but only for a short while. The political purge that followed Stalin's death included what was seen as a serious criticism of how religions and religious institutions were poorly treated. Yet, the official state of scientific atheism continued unchanged and the message of tolerance was slowly eroded, leading to a more vigorous antagonism of religions. As the fierce political struggle for choosing a successor to Stalin ended with the rise of Nikita Khrushchev as the head of the Communist Party and the government, some reforms were introduced. A number of churches were allowed to open and a good number of clergies were hired and put on salaries, becoming government employees and agents of the Communist Party.

Upon my arrival in Moscow, issues of religion or the lack of them had not been among my main concerns. I had no qualms about the absence of religion in the Soviet Union, except for some curiosity about how such a ban had impacted on the population, knowing how much the Russian Orthodox Church had been deeply ingrained in Russian history and the collective population's psyche. Obviously, the incident with my Egyptian anatomist colleague in Kiev, rejecting to do any studies in an atheist country, likely had advanced the issue a bit forward in my mind.

I was born in Egypt to a rather moderately religious Coptic Christian family that observed and followed all Coptic religious traditions, but without the display of any exceptional or noticeably demonstrable religious zeal. Early in my life I developed some antipathy to going to the Sunday church services with my parents. Initially, it was dislike or, precisely, boredom with a rather long service that went on for a few hours, conducted mostly in the Coptic language that the majority of parishioners had not a clue. The priest's sermons were almost the same every week, about sin, punishment and hell, and that did not make much sense to me. My parents' explanation about the very conservative nature of the church adhering to ancient traditions, to survive the religious repressions during the many waves of rulers who occupied Egypt, did not seem to ease my dislike. As I grew up and expanded my knowledge of religions in general, I quickly recognized that my antipathy was not only related to the institution of religion, which in my mind seemed more like a regular corporate entity that was not much different than other corporations, but also I was unable to accept several hallmarks of religion, such as the metaphysical aspects of miracles, divinity and all other science and common sense-defying beliefs. As my outlook on religion expanded, studying other religions and philosophies, I gradually became more tolerant to the concept of religion as a philosophical approach to life, an affiliation with a social group and a means to bolster self-identity. I thought deeply and eventually convinced myself that if I put aside all the mystical and metaphysical inconsistent and unscientific aspects of religions, I could accept all the prophets' teachings, including those of the charismatic preacher Jesus Christ, as they could stand on their own as a valid manifesto and reasonable framework for a respectful and fulfilling life. In that way I felt comfortable not to wage a non-winnable war or protest within myself against religions, and also avoid offending many. I leave the complex theological differences for the experts to argue and debate, but, for myself, religion is a very personal matter that encompasses the many values that I have acquired from various philosophical and religious sources. Would that make me an atheist? I do not believe I am, since I have a strong belief system, though it does not belong to any specific religion or movement. Not becoming isolated in being a "religion of one", I felt comfortable and indeed have benefited from being open to social and personal activities, regardless of the type of religion. After all, the notion of God is nothing more than an idea, rather than a physical presence. As such, every individual can create their own God or Gods.

That brings me back to my experiences in Moscow. As much as the Soviet government and Communist Party's brutal attack on religion and its followers, religion did not completely disappear, it just became submerged. Religion retreated to what it had originally been, a personal experience, except that in the Soviet Union it had to be in secret, for fear of reprisals. As such, it lacked the collective social function, which is one of the benefits from organized groupings. In short, it was not the absence of religion that troubled me most, but the absence of freedom to exercise or pursue a citizen's free will to choose, that had been the most concerning.

One of the questions that then occupied my thinking was whether science can flourish in the absence of religion? The quick response would be "yes, but...". Yes, in the absence of a formal religion, the Soviet Union accomplished a good deal of complex scientific and technical developments, such as the space program and the development of a lethal sophisticated weapons system, but, unfortunately, the benefits from science did not extend to the general population in enriching their life physically or spiritually. Rhetorically, could the presence of religion and a strong church provide a balance in advocating for the population? Unfortunately, the Russian Orthodox church had a long history of misuses and abuses, serving as agents and subservient to the rulers and the powerful, wealthy elites.

The Sculpture of the Madonna and Child
- an era of repression in the Russian Orthodox Church
(Ceramic, hand-painted, 16" x 24")

This glazed ceramic sculpture of The Madonna and Child was acquired from an antique shop in Europe, without any knowledge of its history. We were attracted by its vivid ceramic colours and its artistic values. Subsequent detective research by my wife, Lara, revealed its origins in the Russian Orthodox Church. The sculpture represents a period of internal repression and persecution by the Russian Orthodox Church in the 1600's, of a group of Christians protesting new church reforms. The group separated and became known as the "Old Believers" of the Russian Orthodox Church. Under severe oppression, many of the sect left for Europe and, eventually, several immigrated to Canada. The origin story of this icon was unlocked by close examination of the baby's hands making the "sign of the cross" traditionally, with only two fingers, instead of the reform style of using three fingers.

It is of interest to me that issues related to science and religion have their origin relatively recently, about three hundred years ago, following the development of the era of modern sciences. Prior to that, it was religions and churches who were the ones that fostered scientific interests and developments. Science and knowledge were a source of power and control by validating rules and ideology. A good example was the support of the church for astronomical studies in the sixteenth and seventeenth centuries, motivated by the religious desire to obtain information about the distance between planets, to estimate how wide the heavens were and how many believers could be accommodated. Unfortunately, as science grew much stronger, the churches became fearful and looked at it competitively. The reason I recall such historical anecdotes is that it shows how some aspects of science and religion can be compatible, in spite of the seemingly senseless idea behind the issues of heaven and how many believers it could hold. I believe the modern debate about science and religion has to be reformulated and re-framed using different terms, looking for areas of compatibility rather than what widely separates them. As such, it would be comforting for human beings to have a clear faith and appropriate belief system enhanced by the certainty of science, and the better it would be for progress and the service to humanity.

It is amazing how quickly religion returned to Russia, following the collapse of the Soviet system. It is not only that religion did not completely disappear during the Soviet era, but it also underscored the populations need for some spiritual institutions, like religion. Whether the Russian Orthodox church can reform itself, resurrected in its current powerful role, and serve as an agent for good, is to be seen.

PART IV

Back to Cairo (1964-1968)

Back to the Cairo of Mis-Appointment and Great Disappointment

By the end of 1964, I returned to Cairo - a different Cairo that was overcrowded, more expensive and in the grips of a housing crisis. In the span of just four years the population of Egypt had jumped from a little under twenty million to almost thirty-one million, making it much worse for Cairo, as a result of the mass immigration from the countryside to the large cities. The economy was sluggish and the politics was becoming increasingly tender and complicated, after the government's claim of attempts by the Muslim Brotherhood to overthrow the government. Demonstrations and protests gained a worrisome tone, following the thousands of arrests and jailing of active Muslim Brotherhood leaders, who were identified as the perpetrators and the leaders of the claimed attempts. A new constitution was proposed by President Nasser, which created other political dimensions that added to the boiling political scene in Egypt.

Such was the environment in Egypt upon my return. A meeting with senior officials at the Ministry of Health formally confirmed the rumours I'd heard of placing me in a new position at the Ministry of Health's central laboratories and research facilities, located in a modern building in the fashionable district of Agouza, one of the affluent districts of Cairo. There was no room for negotiations nor any intention to release me from my obligation to serve the government for the next eight years. The previous pre-Moscow plan to join the new academic units of Reproductive Biology and Family Planning at the National Cairo Research Centre did not exist anymore, as the project and its development was still caught in political and financial wranglings. Though I was assured that in the future I'd be supported for a research program and the development of a new neuroendocrine lab, it sounded like pie in the sky, considering the economy's poor state and past unfulfilled similar promises.

My current urgent task, as was emphasized to me so many times, was to run the toxicological clearance program of the imported grains arriving at the ports of Alexandria and Port Said. I was reminded of the great political sensitivity of the matter, in view of the recent extensive riots protesting the government's attempts to raise the price of the heavily subsidized bread, which became by itself one of the main dietary stables in the countryside for both humans and their animals. I was told that the reserve for wheat grain was frequently less than one week, at that time.

Of Bread and Mice - A Tale of Riots, Corruption, Politics and Bad Science

With no other options available at the time, I reluctantly assumed my new position with the Ministry of Health's central laboratories. It was hailed as one of the senior positions at the Ministry of Health, in its modern building that resembled a museum, surrounded by well kept gardens and was the envy of many as a workplace. The position, I was told, had been vacant for some time and the duties were managed by existing senior staff on a short-term basis. I later learned that my arrival had shattered the hopes of many senior staff in being promoted to the position. I also quickly realized the reason for the position being kept vacant for such a long time was due to several pending investigations of significant corruption, that included some previous directors. Anyhow, the welcome was seemingly warm, particularly from the young scientists who were registered at Cairo

University for a Masters or PhD degree, and their expectations of me assisting them.

Reviewing the process of clearance of wheat grains appeared simple, but most complex in its execution, leaving holes for potential misuse and bribes. The grains arrived mostly at the Alexandria sea port that, at that time, lacked any appropriate facility for grain storage and relied only on flat storage called "shona". The grains were stacked in jute bags open to damage, infestations and significant environmental damage and loss. The toxicological clearance took place in Cairo, where a sample of the shipment grain was to be sent in an express sealed parcel to the lab. The clearance was no more than a crude screening, by feeding a group of mice different amounts of grains for seventy-two hours and then comparing the mortality with a control group that was fed the regular diet. Rarely was a sample subjected to any significant biochemical analysis. The results were then communicated by phone to the port in Alexandria and the ship was allowed to unload the grains. The fees charged for a day of waiting in the port was rather expensive and the ship owners were prepared to do anything to expedite the process, to the point of offering incentives (bribes). It was a tedious, crude and unsafe process that clearly did not require a PhD and four years of studies in distant Moscow.

"Of Bread & Mice"

Are you also a volunteer? ...or just for money!!
(A sketch by the author, A.G. Awad, pen on paper 8" x 8")

Realizing my discontent in this complex situation and lacking any better options, I decided to press on, capitalizing on the bit of scientific enthusiasm and discipline left in me. To do a thorough review, I decided to document the major gaps and loopholes, and develop a series of recommendations on how the system could be improved to ensure efficiency and expediency, but also close the gaps that allowed for potential abuse. It took a few months of a scientific search, checking other systems in different international ports, like Marsielle in France or Peres in Greece. Without any fanfare, I quietly handed my report to the Ministry of Health. It included several recommendations, but the two most important were to relocate the process of toxicological clearance closer to where the shipments arrived and develop a lab located within the port itself, such as in

Alexandria, and, secondly, to replace the current inadequate storage facilities with a system of "silos".

What I deliberately omitted from my report was any notion that related to the crux of the problem, which was the over-consumption of wheat, related to the generous subsidy of bread. I recognized that many Egyptians, probably at least thirty to forty percent, were poor or living under the poverty line and they certainly deserved help with the necessities of life, including bread, but not for all Egyptians, who were essentially granted a certain number of loaves per individual on a daily basis. At that time, Egypt was the biggest importer in the world of wheat and also the biggest consumer. One first has to imagine the amount of wheat needed to provide four to five loaves of bread to every citizen and how much all of that amounted to in grain consumption and importation. Over the years, providing subsidized bread became almost a right of the individual. The bread subsidy alone was estimated to consume 0.8-1% of the GDP, a sizable cost that encroached on other priorities. Additionally, the real subtext of such a complex situation was clearly to get a handle on the population explosion that was predicted to surpass one hundred million by the year 2020, which proved to be accurate.

Though I believed that some of my recommendations must have been thought of before, unfortunately, in the current economic and political environment of 1965-1966, they were deemed as extreme. Nasser's proposed new constitution was approved in a referendum and he began his second term as president. Demonstrations and political upheavals continued in parallel with the ongoing court cases for arrested members of the Muslim Brotherhood. A major incident in the small town of Kamshish, in the Nile delta, erupted as tensions were slowly building to a crisis. In May 1966, an official of the Arab Socialist Union (the official government party) was killed in the village of Kamshish while investigating abuses of the Agrarian Reform law, by a wealthy and very influential family there. The incident was quietly interpreted as the result of a continued reactionary and feudal system in rural regions of the country. It resulted in a fierce campaign by the government party against the wealthy and vast land owners and the eventual establishment of the Committee for the Liquidation of Feudalism, which added another layer to the social anxiety and uncertainty. It was hardly an appropriate environment to discuss reforms to the grain clearance system. The need for reforms were acknowledged, but quietly got shelved and abandoned.

A Surprise Confidential Invitation to a Diplomatic Reception

By the summer of 1966, it is hard to say that our life had settled somewhere. My wife, as an engineer and not used to the monotony of the role of a housewife, particularly in Egypt, was lucky to join one of the biggest engineering firms in Egypt and the Middle East, through the connections of one of my relatives to the co-president, the late Professor Michel Bakhum. For myself, my discontent and the feelings of being betrayed by the Egyptian government, I started to look for a post-doctoral position anywhere in Europe, which would give me a legitimate reason to apply for an exit visa. Physicians continued to be prohibited from leaving Egypt without a high-level government permission. Our social and family life became a waiting game for something to come.

Meantime, a delegation from Bani Ayoub, led by Mansour, paid a visit to us in Cairo. It was one of the nicest occasions, but sadly I learned the region had experienced several difficulties, with two physicians filling my position for short periods before each resigning and leaving. Our revived contacts with old friends, including the few writers and artists with whom we kept in contact during the Moscow years, gave us a false sense of deja vu, but, unfortunately, we continued to feel unsettled and imagined how unsatisfying life would be for us if we did not leave Egypt. Among all of these concerns an official letter from the Soviet Embassy in Cairo arrived with an invitation for a reception in October, to celebrate the anniversary of the Bolshevik Revolution. Confidential personal information was requested, which created a heightened anxiety level for us. For one, we were concerned to be on Egypt's Secret Service radar at the Embassy's request for a security clearance, as the protocol dictated. My worry was that I did not, in any shape, want to complicate my wish to eventually leave Egypt. More importantly, in spite of the facade of friendship between the Soviet Union and Egypt, which looked friendly, Egyptian communists or leaning-socialists were still hunted and arrested by the government. Even though I did not belong to either category, and in spite of my attempts to assure myself that the invitation was likely due to my being the first physician to complete graduate studies in the Soviet Union, I did not feel completely assured and almost declined, except for my concern that my wife still carried a Russian passport and needed the Russian Embassy services.

On a warm and pleasant evening in mid-October 1966, we reluctantly joined the reception in the embassy's beautiful gardens on the bank of the Nile, not far from where we lived. The security was obviously tight and officials were visibly in a heightened state of anticipation for the arrival of the guest of honour, no other than President Nasser, and his large entourage. With the high security level, we mingled among the crowd of guests that included known politicians, journalists, writers and the who's who of the cultural and political life in Egypt at that time. The closest one could get to the president, who was huddled around by advisors and his secret service, was at least two to three metres away. President Nasser was impressively tall, with broad but somewhat stooped shoulders, listening most of the time and looking somewhat tired, especially around his eyes. However, what was most visible to me as a physician, was his glowing face, which emitted under the lights a metallic or, specifically, a bronze hue, a very unusual picture that still continues to be vividly recorded in my memory.

It was only one year later, in 1967, that the image returned to me with great significance after the Six Day War, in which miscalculation and poor judgment led Nasser to a spectacular defeat against Israel, who on one early morning in October demolished almost all of the planes of the Egyptian air force. Feeling like all Egyptians and totally crushed by the tragic sad events, I struggled once more with the memory of Nasser's glowing face at the reception a year earlier, and thinking of whether his long sufferings from the rare genetic medical condition, "bronze diabetes", that destroys the liver and the heart, would have impacted on his cognitive abilities and impaired his judgment. A few years later, a confirmation of his bronze diabetes was posted in one of the European newspapers, in a review about Nasser after his death in September 1970. By that time, we were already living in Toronto, Canada, and I had joined the University of Toronto, working in the Department of Pharmacology. A predestined fate that followed an unexpected twist of international events, or maybe it was just being in the right place at the right time and meeting the right persons, as will be described in a later chapter.

PART V

The Post-Doctoral Year
in Rome (1968)

The Career and "Life-Saving" Year at the
Superior Institute of Health, Rome, Italy

The good news arrived in the summer of 1967, after the June disaster of war, in the form of a letter from the Instituto Superiore de Sanita (Institute of Health Research) in Rome, offering me a post-doctoral year at the well-known health research institute in Europe. Our joy was tempered by the concerns of getting the Egyptian government's permission, before I could apply for a visa. Another nerve-racking waiting time had to be endured, amid the utter political confusion in government circles that followed the shocking defeat in June and Nasser's ensuing threat of resignation. Cairo was in a state of disbelief, and the newspapers and streets were filled with the disoriented population pressing Nasser not to resign. Fortunately for me, the government's approval was received. I harboured the idea that the reason for approval was likely related to getting rid of my endless complaints and frequent criticism that troubled more than a few senior bureaucrats. It was fine with me, whatever the reason, as I finally got my visa to go to Rome. However, I wondered whether the invitation to the diplomatic reception and the security clearance I had received the year before may have expedited the visa process, which usually took a long time.

As I headed to the Cairo airport at 5 a.m. to catch my very early morning flight to Rome, I made every possible precaution not to betray my secret intentions of not returning to Egypt. My luggage was minimal, appearing to be enough for a trip of only a few weeks, and my wife and our baby son would join me later. It was a strange, but very emotional event, slipping away unnoticed from the country of my birth. Yet, in spite of all the difficulties and disappointments I encountered during my short stay in Cairo, I felt sad for the ominously stalled country I left behind.

Arriving in Rome very early in the morning, I took a taxi to the Instituto Superiore de Sanita, on the well-known street Viale Regina Elena, just opposite the campus of Rome's university. No one was there at such an early time of the day, but the security guard, knowing nothing about me, took me to the office of the director, Professor Marino Bettolo, whom I discovered starts his day as early as 7 a.m. It was an unplanned, but pleasant welcoming meeting. He gave me a few details about the Institute and its activities, and, learning that I had just arrived from the airport with my luggage and that it was my first time in Rome, he decided that I should take a couple of days to settle in and get familiar with the city. Among all of his kind suggestions, he strongly advised me to read the English translation of the famous book L'Italiene (the Italians) by the famous Italian writer Luigi Barzini, which he suggested would help me to understand and enjoy life in Rome. It was a very helpful and encouraging start to my studies. I was then driven in the Institute's car to where I would be temporarily staying, finally arriving at the International Foreign Students Hostel, known by its initials as CIVIS, which was originally built to house athletes attending the Rome Olympic games a few years earlier.

In a few days, after a badly needed rest, I returned to the Institute to a friendly welcome from my Italian supervisor, Professor Amelio Carpi and his deputy Dotoressa (Doctor for women) Carla Cartoni. Professor Carpi was the head of the Laboratory of Therapeutic Chemistry, which was not far from the laboratory of the internationally known Professor Rita Levi-Montalcini, who was awarded the Nobel Prize in Physiology in 1986. In 1968, and throughout my post-doctoral year, Professor Levi-Montalcini was away in the USA, serving as a visiting professor at Washington University in St. Louis, Missouri. However, learning about her life-story and how she survived as a Jewish scientist during the fascist Mussolini regime, I was deeply touched by her immense courage, determination and resilience in the face of all odds; qualities I felt deeply in need of in confronting my critical decision not to return to Cairo and search for a new career.

In a couple of weeks, my training plans were settled as I joined Dotoressa Cartoni in her planned study of "Stress and Cardiovascular Reactivity", a topic close to my very interests and which certainly complemented my previous experiences in Moscow. The design was experimental on adrenalectomized Wistar rats and testing the effects of various corticosteroid medications on the response of splanchnic nerve stimulation. Initially, the schedule looked a bit relaxed, with a few coffee breaks a day and also a couple of hours in the early afternoon for the famous Italian siesta. Mistakenly, I had worried about whether such a relaxed schedule would allow for the completion of the study before the end of my post-doctoral year. Time proved me wrong, as the majority of the staff worked long hours into the evening. In the end, the project was accomplished on time and a manuscript was prepared before my departure at the end of the year, and actually got published quickly in the journal Archives Internationales de Pharmacodynamie et de Therapie.

Life in Rome in 1968 was rather politically turbulent, with frequent demonstrations and violent clashes between the radical left "Red Brigades" and the ultra right, mostly religious groups. It was a dangerous time that culminated in the tragic assassination of the Prime Minister Aldo Moro. On the other hand, the streets and squares in Rome were somewhat entertaining, filled with music and songs of protest, drugs and all the fringe demonstrations of the 1960s era. As the summer approached, tensions in Europe were mounting everywhere, including Prague in Czechoslovakia, which was besieged with demonstrations pressing for freedom to get out of the orbit of the Soviet block. Many expected that a violent Russian confrontation would follow. As the politics became imminently threatening, many Czechoslovakians post-doctoral Fellows, training like me at the Institute in Rome, decided to accept the offer by Canada to accommodate them, in case they decided not to return to Czechoslovakia. Many of them took up the offer. Our next-door neighbours in the building in which we lived, Dr. Karel Cocandrle and his wife, Anna, who was a medical student, were two of our few friends in Rome and had decided to interrupt their training and accepted positions at the University of Alberta, in Edmonton, Canada. They maintained correspondence with us and urged us to consider a career in Canada, as they seemed happy with their new life.

By mid-November 1968, Karel connected us with a professor of endocrinology at the University of Alberta, who was recruiting for a new position in the soon to open Medical School at the University of Calgary, in Alberta, Canada. In short, after a number of exchanges by mail, and with serious hesitation on my part, I tentatively agreed to consider an offer to join the new Department of Medicine at the University of Calgary, with the promise of funding for the establishment of an experimental lab and a program in neuro-endocrinology. Once more, my ambition to study and work in London was curtailed and rerouted to Canada. I experienced a sigh of some relief, but felt a palpable anxiety, as I was again about to fly into the unknown. At that time there were no direct flights from Europe to Calgary, so we booked a flight with a few days stop-over in Toronto and, as is frequently said, the rest is history. A short stop-over in Toronto has lasted over fifty years, and instead of the University of Calgary as my place of work and academia, it shifted to the University of Toronto.

Interlude

The stop-over in Toronto that lasted for fifty-years
- Destiny or just meeting the right person,
in the right place, at the right time

Arriving in Toronto for a stop-over of a few days before continuing travel to Calgary, the city was blanketed by fresh snow and the weather was frigid and reminiscent of Moscow's winters, except for one major difference; by the next day, the snow was almost completely cleared away from the streets by the city. The Japanese Canadian landlady, who accommodated us for a few nights on the second floor of her very comfortable, old Victorian house on Palmerston Avenue, not far from the campus of the University of Toronto, was very welcoming and pleasant. Although we had several contacts in Alberta and British Columbia, we knew no one in Toronto, except for the one name and contact that was provided to us by a few of the professors in Rome, in case we needed advice or directions. The name of our only contact in Toronto was that of Professor Edward Schonbaum. His wife, Marie Louise, was also a professor, both of them with the Department of Pharmacology at the University of Toronto.

I am not sure if it was just an act of curiosity or me subconsciously experiencing the possibility of other alternatives at the University of Toronto, the largest and most well-known university in Canada, but I decided to take a walk and look for Professor Schonbaum, and I was lucky enough to have the opportunity of meeting him. After several back-and-forth introductory questions about my background and future plans, he kindly offered to introduce me to Professor Edward Sellers, the Chair of the Department of Pharmacology, who at the time was also serving as the Associate Dean of the Faculty of Medicine. Luck worked once more, as Professor Sellers happened to be available. I responded to almost the same background queries. After about twenty minutes, he stood up and with a very encouraging smile said, "You really should stay here. We need someone with a background like yours and we have a job for you to coordinate a major project that is funded by the Medical Research Council. In two years you can go to Calgary, if you still wish to then". He stressed that he would deal with any issues arising with the University of Calgary, as it turned out that he well knew the Chair of the Department of Medicine at the new university. It was a huge surprise that intuitively appealed to me on the spot, and Professor Seller's persuasive kindness made it much easier to affirm my immediate interest. It was another case of "a bird in the hand..." and I accepted, rather than waiting for the unknown in Calgary and, particularly, the dreaded severity of the Calgary winters had been one of my major concerns. With that, I was introduced to the Department's secretary, Mrs. Morrison, to deal with the paperwork and her advice about practical matters, such as how and where to rent an apartment close to public transportation and the cheaper way to furnish the apartment using the facilities of the biggest bargain store and Toronto landmark, "Honest Ed's", which was close to the university campus.

Walking back to share the news with my wife, I felt pleasantly a bit light-headed by the swiftness of the events and my quick response, which conferred at last an element of certainty that I had been missing in the last couple of months, brooding over various career plans and even more-so about what to expect in Calgary. Within a few days I was already on the job, struggling to put the multicentre neuro-endocrine/thyroid research project back on track. It was a great opportunity to get to know the senior investigators of the seven participating academic endocrinology programs in Toronto and be able to attend their bi-weekly research rounds. Over a short time my academic responsibilities were extended to supervising medical students and graduate researchers for Master's degrees. In less than fifteen months the large study was completed, data analyzed and a manuscript was ready to send to the prestigious medical journal The Lancet, under the title of: Long-Acting Thyroid Stimulator in Graves' Disease. It was published in August 1970, which was a big prize to me, being the first major publication for me in Canada, as well as the pride it brought with the affirmation of my academic and research experiences and potential.

Our life in Toronto seemed to settle comfortably, as the concerns we initially developed about life in Toronto, which at first appeared to us as mostly a provincial city, started to slowly change, becoming more of a cosmopolitan metropolis that rivalled the more European city of Montreal in French Canada. Yet, the issue that I continued to struggle with was my long-term future career plans, which became more pressing with the passage of time, along with the increased knowledge and impressions that one gains over time. A few issues became much clearer, thanks to the frank and candid discussions with my boss and mentor, Professor Sellers. Making a career dependent on research carried a good deal of risk and instability related to the instability at that time of external research funding, an opinion that was supported by several of my university colleagues. Pursuing a career as a clinician scientist is more rewarding financially, particularly in my case, starting a career anew in Canada at age thirty-six, which meant I lost about ten years of earning that already went for my PhD and the extra experiences as a post-doctoral fellow in Rome. More fundamentally, I felt as a clinician, I would miss very much the clinical and human contacts that I valued and was also good at. Additionally, my wife and I didn't want to move away from Toronto, a city that in a short couple of years felt like home to us.

With all of these concerns, I decided to look for avenues to gain an academic medical specialty that would become the clinical home-base for continuing my neuroscience research. To do that I needed to have a medical license in order to be able to engage in a medical practice. In the midst of all these questions and requirements an opportunity suddenly materialized through an unplanned encounter with Professor Harvey Stancer, who regularly attended the bi-weekly thyroid research rounds. At that time, Professor Stancer was developing a new biological psychiatry program in Toronto, sharing with Professor Harvey Moldofsky as co-directors of a specialized clinical investigative unit in what then was the well-known Clarke Institute of Psychiatry (currently the Centre for Addiction and Mental Health, CAMH). It was an intriguing opportunity from Professor Stancer, who persuaded me to move and join the University of Toronto's academic Department of Psychiatry.

The timing in the early 1970s was right. Not withstanding my early antipathy to psychiatry during my medical studies in the late 1940s, the image and the practice of psychiatry in the early 1970s was different and had gained much more substance and respectability. The psychoanalytic concepts that dominated the practice of psychiatry for decades was in its waning years, rapidly being displaced by the introduction of Chlorpromazine and the advances in the modern neuropsycho-pharmacology that followed. Advances in the neurosciences had made significant inroads in a deeper understanding of the neurochemistry and neurobiology of the brain. It was a great and promising time for psychiatry, representing one of the few high peaks of scientific progress among the many low valleys of frequent stagnation that followed. In the end, a decision was not difficult, particularly as it provided the opportunity for psychiatry and my neuroscience background training to finally come together. In addition, migrating to psychiatry and completing the requirements for obtaining a specialist status would guarantee me receiving a license to practice. Fortunately, because of my PhD and post-graduate research training, I was granted a shorter time requirement for training in psychiatry.

The process got quickly underway by meeting with the Director of Postgraduate Training in Psychiatry, Professor Vivian Rakoff, a psychiatrist, psychoanalyst and prolific writer. The meeting was pleasant and included a few personal moments about surviving my years in Moscow, life in Cairo and the 1948 Israel Independence War, in which he had participated as a volunteer. At the end of our interview, for some reason he brought up the issue of homosexuality in the Middle East, which perplexed me, in the context of the other issues discussed. It brought to mind an interesting cartoon I noticed in the New Yorker a few years earlier, about a psychiatrist and a psychoanalyst meeting in the corridor and greeting each other with "Good morning, Professor", leaving each of them thinking, "I wonder what he meant!". Anyhow, over the many years that followed, as we got to know each other very well, I never asked him what he meant at that time in 1971, at our introductory meeting. A brief, but pleasant meeting with Professor Robin Hunter, the Chair of the Academic Department of Psychiatry followed. It's likely he was one of the last in the era of psychoanalysts, serving as Chair of major academic Departments of Psychiatry in Canada, and signalling the growing shift in the field towards the rising of psycho-neurobiology trends and the waning of the psychoanalytic doctrines that had populated major academic departments for decades.

I felt welcomed everywhere, but with occasional curiosity by some colleagues regarding my having started psychiatry at the relatively older age of thirty-six, compared to colleagues who joined psychiatry soon after graduation. In retrospect, I believe the years I spent in Moscow, Cairo and Rome added something more than knowledge, in terms of maturity, confidence and being comfortable in dealing with diversities and also adversities.

I was fortunate to spend my introductory year in psychiatry in the Clinical Investigation Unit at the Clarke Institute of Psychiatry, supervised by two of the top psychobiological psychiatrists, "the two Harveys", as they were called; Professor Harvey Stancer and Professor Harvey Moldofsky. Professor Stancer had his major focus on mood disorders, while Professor Moldofsky focused on neurophysiological disorders, with special expertise in sleep disorders. He also maintained a particular interest on the rather uncommon condition of Tourette's syndrome, which quickly brought to mind the surprise encounter I had in 1951 with Madam E.K., who most likely was suffering from Tourette's syndrome.

Working in the Clinical Psychiatric Investigation Unit was a great learning and challenging experience. Patients admitted there came from all over the province of Ontario, and, by the nature of their diagnostic and/or treatment challenges, the Clinical Investigation Unit was almost the end of the road for getting help. The thorough and detailed systematic approach to diagnosis and management based on an individualized strategy proved very useful to the majority of such complex presentations. Realizing the limits of available psychiatric treatments, every admitted patient who hadn't accomplished a significant symptomatic improvement was discharged at least with a clear diagnosis and long-term plans for further management.

One of the vexing issues was dealing with severe complex patients, who were unresponsive to treatment and became a casualty of suicide, even with the most strict precautions. Such unfortunate situations had troubled me for some time, asking the question over and over; could we had averted such a tragic incident? One could easily lose perspective and self-confidence, and even drop out of psychiatric training altogether. The emotional impact on the physician can be as devastating as that of families. What counts most at these times was the support the physician gets from the supervisor and colleagues, which I received from both of my supervisors, as well as from Dr. Paul Garfinkel, who at that time was the Chief Resident and a colleague in the Clinical Investigation Unit. Unfortunately, the psychiatric training curricula usually includes teaching about the approach to be taken with families, but virtually nothing or very little about the impact on physicians and how to deal with such tragic situations. Every psychiatrist learns quickly that the issue of suicide is part and parcel of psychiatric practice and, particularly, that not every act of suicide is preventable. Yet, its emotional impact on the physician is serious and can be long-lasting, especially in a training situation. Since the physician trainee is delegated the responsibility of managing patients who originally are the supervisor's patients, a feeling of betrayal of the supervisor's trust can be demoralizing and add to the emotional impact, complicating it by the additional feelings of guilt. Overall, the total experience working in the Clinical Psychiatric Investigation Unit was valuable, both professionally and academically. Through the extensive contacts of the supervisors, one got quickly introduced to the national scene of psychiatry in Canada.

One of the interesting events at that time was the strained relationship between academia, including the Department of Psychiatry at the University of Toronto and the pharmaceutical industry. That was the time of big pharma, the introduction of blockbuster brands, the highly competitive marketing approaches and high profitability. The pharmaceutical industry appeared keen on co-opting academia in their, at times, unethical marketing schemes, and academia was equally desperate for funding of research and education, which inevitably ended in a collision course that undermined any collaborative efforts. The conflict proved to be more serious for psychiatry, in view of the historically low funding for psychiatry and mental health. With his forward-thinking, and seizing on the opportunity, Professor Stancer decided to challenge both academia and the pharmaceutical industry by inviting the medical directors of the major national and international pharmaceutical companies to Canada, to a major all-day meeting arranged at the Clark Institute of Psychiatry.

The meeting was billed as; let us talk "not under the table", but openly over the table. Grievances were stated from both sides, which boiled down to a simple statement: Universities like to get support from the pharmaceutical industry, but deny them any notion of partnership. The meeting was remarkably successful in its candid exchange of how to resolve the areas of conflict. I was quite pleased with my participation and the invitation of Professor Stancer. The meeting did manage to set a new course for a collaborative relationship between academic psychiatry and the pharmaceutical industry that soon contributed to the national efforts for the establishment of the Canadian College of Neuropsychopharmacology (CCNP) in 1978. I was both proud and honoured years later to be elected as its president in 1993, for two years, and in 2000 I was awarded the CCNP Medal that honours meritorious career and outstanding contributions to neuropsychopharmacology nationally and internationally.

My next assignment was at the Queen Street Psychiatric Hospital, generally known as "999 Queen Street". The hospital was in a major transition and most of its old buildings, erected in 1850, were demolished and replaced by two modern buildings on the east and west ends of the extensive grounds, each serving a geographical catchment area that corresponded with the east or west ends of the city of Toronto. The new buildings, by the standards of 1970, were considered "ultra modern", providing for the first time single room accommodation, with private toilet and shower facilities. It was interesting that some patients felt uncomfortable in their modern single accommodation, because they missed the company and the communal living of the old big wards.

When I joined the facility in 1973, the large central building was still standing, but awaiting demolition and the last stage of reconstruction that included a modern swimming pool and a large gym. The old building where I worked, though dilapidated, betrayed signs of its former beautifully constructed architectural design; huge halls with glass windows from floor to ceiling, and the beautiful decorative features that the high ceilings still retained. The living accommodations were based on large wards that held more than thirty patients. One central hall served as the communal focal point of the large clinical facility and was constantly crowded with patients and staff, virtually in perpetual motion most of the day, particularly at medication time when the patients lined up to receive their medications.

The senior psychiatrist, and my supervisor, was British-trained Professor Sebastian Littman, who was a wonderful and highly experienced teacher and one of the few academic psychiatrists widely knowledgeable about the foundational history of psychiatry and its contributors. He was an authority on Karl Jaspers, the German Swiss psychiatrist, philosopher and prolific writer. Though Karl Jasper's contribution was not that widely known or taught in Toronto, Professor Littman introduced Karl Jaspers to a wider audience of trainees, psychiatrists and many others in philosophy and social sciences. Through his many weekly seminars he reviewed Jaspers' contributions to psychiatry, phenomenology and philosophy, with particular focus on Jaspers' major contribution; the textbook of General Psychopathology.

"Seb", as Professor Littman preferred to be called by everyone, had a unique sense of humour, which was his way of dealing with the many daily complex issues inherent in running a modern psychiatric program in an ancient asylum. One time, during my supervisory session with him, we talked about the deafening noise and the large crowds in the central hall, which in many ways looked like the busy Union Station in downtown Toronto. He quipped that it was difficult in such a crowd to recognize who was a patient or a staff. To test such an observation, we arranged to show up very early the next morning at the time of medication dispensation, and both of us sat in a couple of chairs among the long line of chairs arranged against the wall. Sure enough, many staff passed by us without noticing the presence of the Chief Psychiatrist in charge of that program. It may have been a funny story that spoke volumes about how chaotic life and practice were in the old asylums, but at the same time it showed the importance of creating enough communal space for patients to congregate and interact in the modern restructuring of the asylum that shouldn't be missed. Overall, my experiences at 999 Queen Street were positive and highly educational, putting me daily face-to-face with the disturbed and weird world of psychosis and the uncontrolled and expansive world of manics, the real and major psychiatric disorders. I believe it was there that I likely developed my early academic interest in dealing with psychotic disorders.

The year passed quickly and I had to leave for my final six-month rotation that I chose to spend with one of the most knowledgeable and respected academic neuropsychiatrists and phenomenologists, Professor Alexander Bonkalo. I was truly fortunate to have had such a unique opportunity, as he was always over-subscribed, particularly in view of the lack of teaching of phenomenology in other academic settings. Professor Bonkalo was originally from Hungary, but migrated to Canada following the 1956 Hungarian uprising and the Russian invasion of Hungary. I used to meet with him weekly, benefiting from his expertise of psychopathology. Our discussions dealt extensively with issues related to phenomenology, which has now almost disappeared from most psychiatric training curricula in the USA and Canada.

It was very interesting that as early as 1973, during the time I spent with Professor Bonkalo, the gradual loss of interest in teaching phenomenology had already been noticed. Though there may have been several reasons that contributed to such a decline in the interest of psychiatric phenomenology, which I will discuss in more detail in a later chapter, it is clear that there was a determined effort in the early 1970s towards objective and standardized observations and diagnosis, in order to move psychiatry into a scientific discipline, possibly playing a major role in accentuating the demise of phenomenology. The very nature of phenomenology represented the personal and subjective experiences of patients, which at that time was not measurable or quantifiable to qualify as scientific, an area that a few years later proved to be incorrect as we introduced valid and reliable methods to measure patients' subjective experiences and how they felt on antipsychotic medications.

In six months, my training requirement was completed and the challenge then was to secure a job in my new role as a psychiatrist. As happened many times before, I had just started to look around for what was available and received an invitation letter. It came from Dr. Ian Bond, the medical director of the Lakeshore Psychiatric Hospital in the west end of Toronto, asking me to join them. Once more, a bird in the hand...etc. was the modus operandi as I quickly accepted, most likely or at least in part somewhat intrigued by my curiosity to see what had happened to the concept of the mental asylum since my experiences some twenty years earlier in the Abbassiya Mental Asylum in Cairo.

PART VI

The Final Stop – Toronto, Canada (1969)

The Beginning of Fifty Years of Academic Psychiatry with Schizophrenia as a Major Focus

The Lakeshore Psychiatric Hospital – The Hospital Built by Its Patients, Moral Work Therapy or Coercive Exploitation

In 1974, I was recruited by Dr. Ian Bond, the new Director of the Lakeshore Psychiatric Hospital, who had taken over in 1972, from the retiring Superintendent, Dr. Ronald Gun. Dr. Gun not only was the last to carry the title of "Superintendent", which was the designation given by the British colonial authorities in all of their colonies. Dr. Gun was also the last superintendent to live with his family in the well-designed residence on the hospital grounds, next to the school.

The hospital was built in 1888, as an extension of the deteriorated and overcrowded Provincial Lunatic Asylum in Toronto, known to this day as "999 Queen Street". The history of the development of Lakeshore Psychiatric Hospital, in New Toronto, included a rather unique situation by which patients from the Provincial Lunatic Asylum shared in many aspects of the construction process. Many of these patients were eventually transferred to the new hospital after its official opening in 1889. It is not clear how the patients were selected to participate in the construction and whether they were given a choice or consented. One presumes, at least, that they were physically capable of doing the work, recognizing that the resident population in 1888 at 999 Queen Street West included a good number of jail inmates. Nevertheless, just the appearance of the situation introduces a number of ethical and moral challenges. Indeed, such concerns did arise during the course of the construction. Clearly, if such a situation had arisen in modern times, it would have been dealt with according to the ethical framework well-established in mental health legislation and well-grounded in the doctrine of informed consent. On the other hand, the question that needs to be addressed first is whether, at the present time, are we entitled to judge such a situation according to our current ethical framework, more than eighty years later? To address the issue, one needs to examine it in the context of psychiatric care in the 1880s, and also take into consideration the societal conditions of that time.

The major health event of the mid-nineteenth century had been the development in 1850 of the Provincial Lunatic Asylum at 999 Queen Street West. It was a monumental event in its psychiatric goals of providing more appropriate housing and treatment of mentally ill patients in Toronto, who were scattered among various jails and gaols. Architecturally, under the design of the famous architect John Howard, the building in its neoclassic Victorian style was hailed as a monument of enlightenment, consistent with the quest for moral therapy and, as such, it served as a representation of British imperial accomplishment. In contrast to the initial glory of the building, it soon became over-crowded and deteriorated, lacking any effective therapeutic approaches, meaning recidivism and chronicity, which became a dominant feature of so many residents.

At some point, some 250 patients were deemed incurable, which became the impetus behind the emerging idea of developing another facility to accommodate the "incurables". Mixed with such a notion was the concern regarding the appalling overcrowded conditions and the evolving belief that living in a home-like condition, with

113

fresh air, greenery and a beautiful environment, could favourably impact mental illness. Such thinking was advanced by the powerful superintendent of the Provincial Lunatic Asylum, Dr. Joseph Workman. He also popularized the idea of work and recreational approaches that could serve as antidotes for mental illness. Indeed, patients of the asylum were assigned serving roles in maintenance and upkeep, as well as in construction. The archive clearly documents that the wall surrounding the 999 Queen Street asylum was basically built by patients. Parts of it along the east side and on Shaw Street continue to exist as a heritage site. Patients were not paid and were expected to participate in various chores, whether coerced or not is not very clear, except that the archive includes some complaints from patients about hours of work and a few written requests to be payed for the work they provided.

In essence, then, though one can make a case for some exploitation, patient participation was framed in terms of therapy, in the absence of any other effective therapeutic agents. To add to the complexity of the issue, the dwindling financial support by the provincial government furthered the need to involve patients in the maintenance of the institution, from cleaning, laundry, carpentry, gardening, etc., in order to save funds. By modern-day standards, patients should have been clearly consenting and compensated, at least, nominally, as it would have been impossible to pay them the regular rates.

Overall, though I do believe that the questions raised about ethics and morality, even as a therapy, needs to be raised, at the same time we need not be harsh in our judgment, putting the issue appropriately in the context of the psychiatric conditions at that time and the availability of resources. Practically speaking, I tend to believe, at least for some patients, working in the construction of the new Lakeshore Psychiatric Hospital took them for a while away from the stagnant and deplorable living conditions at the 999 Queen Street mental asylum.

The Lakeshore Psychiatric Hospital was designed by well-known architects and famous landscapers of the time, and according to the new model referred to as the "cottage style", that was strongly advocated by the Superintendent of 999 Queen Street, Dr. Joseph Workman. The idea was grounded in the notion of moral therapy which provided a quiet environment, surrounded by landscaped parks that were thought to be more conducive for recovery. Instead of one large institutional building, the hospital was designed as nine pods, each accommodating 120 to 140 patients. The four Victorian style pods that faced Lake Ontario were for women patients, and later included an adolescent unit. The other five pods were for men, each one designated to cover a geographical catchment area. The construction of the nine pods, as well as the central administrative building and the service and utility buildings were mostly constructed by patients as part of their work therapy, a notion that raised a good deal of ethical concerns, as already discussed.

By the time the hospital opened in 1889, it included a farm run by the patients, under supervision, a school, a cricket field, a villa as residence for the superintendent and even its own cemetery, where patients who had lived most of their life there were buried. Even the coffins were made by the patients themselves. From the outside of the different buildings and the later added community hall, contributed by the City of Toronto, it looked like a resort facing the lake and surrounded by lush green, landscaped gardens.

Yet, by 1974, when I joined the hospital, the inside of the pods were appalling and urgently required massive renovations. The units were already overcrowded and the initial concept of the serene and quiet environment conducive for recovery was already gone. The almost 80-year history of the hospital, from its original name as Mimico Branch Asylum to the subsequent many name changes, finally becoming Lakeshore Psychiatric Hospital, certainly reflected the evolving attitudes towards psychiatry and mental health. Low-level government funding added to the over-use and abuse of the limited space, contributing to a noticeable deterioration that required massive and urgent renovations at a time of an economic crunch for the provincial government that had to deal with several other priorities.

My responsibility as a senior psychiatrist was to ensure the provision of psychiatric care in the defined catchment area that included the rapidly developing west end of Toronto, as well as both the Boroughs of York and Etobicoke. I have to say that in spite of all of the deterioration, I was proud and most appreciative for the psychiatric teams that included a few psychiatrists, a general medical physician, nurses, social workers, a psychologist and an occupational therapist, who were all collegial and collaborated in the provision of care for seriously psychiatrically ill patients in a most unhelpful and poor physical working environment. Yet, the degree of enthusiasm was palpable among everyone, infused by the high-spirit, hope and optimism for the new era of psychiatry that was ushered in less than ten years before, following the introduction of the antipsychotic chlorpromazine.

True, cracks started to dim a bit of the rosy picture of modern psychiatry, as several patients disliked chlorpromazine and the other newer medications that followed, like haloperidol. Several patients began taking their medications irregularly or stopped taking them altogether, leading to multiple relapses and hospitalizations. As much as we recognized the inconvenience of the many side-effects, particularly the subtle subjective feelings of unease, dysphoria and feeling like zombies, we had no better alternative. Although we were able to provide some supportive care, it proved difficult for many patients residing far away in the Borough of York to commute frequently over a long distance to attend supportive group care at the hospital campus, and there were no funds to consider developing an outpost clinic in the Borough of York. Fortunately, and somehow miraculously, even though I am not a believer of miracles, I was asked on behalf of the hospital to attend a meeting in the Borough of York with the late Donald Cameron MacDonald, a past member of the Ontario Legislature, who for years represented the Borough of York South. It was a memorable meeting event with a remarkable and creative thinker that left me enthused and optimistic.

The York Multi-Service Community Centre - A Tribute to the Late Donald Cameron MacDonald

One of the most inspiring and enjoyable tasks among my other responsibilities, both clinical and administrative, was the attendance of the regular monthly meeting of the community board of directors of the newly developed York Multi-Service Community Centre, representing Lakeshore Psychiatric Hospital. The creative idea and the driving force behind the development of such a new one-stop medical, psychiatric, social and legal health care centre belonged to the vision of the Honourable Donald C. MacDonald. He was a member of the Ontario Legislature, representing for number of years the Borough of York South. He also had been the driving force for the development of the New Democratic Party, from the ashes of the Social Democratic Co-operative Commonwealth Federation. He also was an inspiring advocate for political and social reforms, with a keen focus on prison reforms and universal health care. In my first meeting with him, he impressed me by his infective enthusiasm and also by his clear understanding of the social challenges and the various political barriers blocking efforts for change. Hence, arose his new idea of how to improve access to psychiatric care, by including the supportive services that were needed to accomplish comprehensive care under one roof and much closer to where the patients lived. Around the large board table were several members of participating partners and agencies, both governmental and private, such as Unemployment and Social Welfare, Legal Aid, the John Howard Society, Family and Child Services, Children's Aid Society and hospitals providing medical and psychiatric care to the residents of the Borough of York, including Lakeshore Psychiatric Hospital. All were organized under one roof. Truly, it was a new and bold idea, to be able to get commitments from such diverse agencies that generally operated mostly on their own. As for Lakeshore Psychiatric Hospital, the hospital contributed by seconding one mental health nurse and one social worker, in addition to the regular services of the hospital as a back up for hospitalization and outpatient clinics. Modelled on the one-stop shopping successfully introduced by the retail business sector, the York Multi-Service Centre became a success story, not only as a result of its integrative approach and access to services, but also as an information and public education resource for the York region. Backed by the political activism of Donald C. MacDonald, the York Multi-Service Centre provided a successful integrative model at a time when the care for psychiatric patients and their need to access several supporting agencies was fragmented, time consuming and poorly coordinated.

With the government closure of Lakeshore Psychiatric Hospital in 1979, and the transfer of the hospital patients and programs to 999 Queen Street West, the Ontario Provincial Psychiatric Hospital, the York Multi-Service Centre psychiatric contributions continued to be provided and expanded by opening a store-front mini-centre to serve the Parkdale area, the district that became crowded with the many discharged chronic psychiatric patients from the nearby old asylum. Unfortunately, over the years and as a result of the frequent economic constraints, though the basic concept of such innovative thinking had somehow survived, several agencies had to scale down or withdraw their services under the pressure of budgetary cuts. In recent years, the concept of one-stop care has been taken over more so by the government, in a reduced structure and a more limited model that still continues in some parts of the City of Toronto.

I do believe the pioneering efforts of the late Donald C. MacDonald and his colleagues, who created and implemented such a visionary model of integrated patient-centred care, has demonstrated its feasibility and its usefulness. I believe that the need for such integrative models are required even more now, particularly with the increased care demands of a rapidly increasing senior population. My hope, at present, is that such integrative and innovative models, or newer versions of them, can serve as the basis for reshaping the provision of new psychiatric services. It would be a major tribute to Donald C. MacDonald, who by his enthusiasm, charisma and devotion to help has opened the door for a better approach to serve our patients close to where they live.

Back to the New "999 Queen Street" Hospital

In 1976, I accepted my new appointment as the Psychiatrist Director of the rather large Southwestern Psychiatric Services, in the newly rebuilt Ontario Provincial Psychiatric Hospital in Toronto, popularly known as "999 Queen Street". The geographical catchment area extended from downtown Toronto and westward to the border of the City of Mississauga, including the boroughs of Etobicoke and York. My position involved extensive administrative and clinical responsibilities, and as an Associate Professor at the University of Toronto's academic Department of Psychiatry, my role was to promote and implement the university agenda in education and research.

My return to "999 Queen Street Hospital" after three years since I was last there, marked the beginning of the last phase of reconstruction of the hospital. The central building, where I spent my year with Professor Littman, had already been demolished, giving way to the construction of a third building, to house the Northern Clinical Services that would cover most of the northern regions of the City of Toronto. The Southwestern Psychiatric Services building, which was to become my work home for the next four years, included five large clinical programs housed in its five floors. The first floor was occupied by the Crisis and Acute Care Unit, plus the Administration Office and the Outpatient Clinic. The second to the fourth floors were occupied by clinical programs that accommodated patients grouped according to the level of care required. The fifth floor held the title of the "Revolving Door" program, which was distinct in the type of patients admitted there.

Most of the patients admitted or transferred to the fifth floor were young and given the diagnosis of psychosis or, specifically, schizophrenia, with many of them also receiving the frequent diagnosis of comorbid drug abuse. Most of the patients were well-known to the staff by their frequent and brief admissions, and by their fierce resistance to taking medications. They were known as the "anti-medication" group, who disliked or almost hated to take medications. They frequently complained that antipsychotic medications made them more sick and unable to feel or function. As soon as they were stabilized and became uncertifiable, and we were unable to keep them against their wish, they discharged themselves against medical advice. They rarely attended follow-up clinics and were not seen again until their next relapse, falling once more into a serious psychotic state, and so on and on. The story went round and round, landing them quickly in chronicity and total disability. It was a challenging program that dealt with challenging patients, and with no other options for treatment except to basically push the hated medications.

That was the state of the Revolving Door program, until a few tragic events took place within eight months of me assuming my position. Within a short period of six months, three patients committed suicide, one after another. They were not only tragic and sad events, but also very challenging, in terms of why the patients hated taking medications to the point that they took their own life. As will be detailed in a later chapter, the three tragic events triggered an intense search to understand the cause, and took until almost thirty years later of a continued search to uncover the major reasons behind it. Meanwhile, my original plans for reforming psychiatric care was resumed, including major programmatic changes to the Revolving Door program by enhancing behavioural approaches, as well as a regular review of medications, as part of the patients' and families'-centred program to enhance medication compliance behaviour.

I was very fortunate to have a good complement of well-trained staff that included nurses, social workers, psychologists, occupational and art therapists, as well as a resident chaplain, a visiting rabbi and an imam. Every program had at least one to two psychiatrists and a number of psychiatric residents-in-training, in addition to nursing, social work, psychology and occupational-therapy students. An in-house medical general practitioner attended to medical issues, including preparation for electroconvulsive therapy (ECT). With my style of management, which I called "democratic participatory management", the administrative staff were comfortable and at ease in handling the many serious issues related to psychiatric practices. I worked hard to keep a reasonable and harmonious balance among the diverse professionals, and between the program and government bureaucracy. My four years in charge of such complex clinical services certainly proved to be a productive experience, clinically and academically.

Clinically, we introduced a system of "psychiatric audits" that targeted specific clinical topics or addressed observed clinical gaps and other emerging deficits. We established regular case reviews and presentations, as well as monitored length-of-stay, in order to create a reasonable turnover that could facilitate in dealing with the frequent pressures for beds. The research program that followed the tragic suicides of the three patients, cemented the most challenging psychiatric disorder of schizophrenia as our, and my, major academic focus. A few other significant interests also developed, including the complex issue of quality of care in psychiatry and its evaluation, which culminated in the organization of a first-of-its-kind symposium in 1979, with its proceedings published in a book of the same title, "Evaluation of Quality of Care in Psychiatry", which will be further highlighted in a later chapter.

With all the challenges and responsibilities, the work environment was cordial, friendly and based on mutual trust and respect. There were moments that were exceptionally hilarious and funny, like the time the Chaplin conducted a wedding ceremony for two of the staff under a huge oak tree at the front of the building, that frequently provided a serene ambience and shade for summer picnics. The wedding was attended by the staff and a number of patients, demonstrating a well-cohesive community spirit. Since then, weddings under the oak tree have become almost an institutional tradition.

For me, personally, at last my old "interest" in the area of arts, which was dormant for years during my many travels and dislocations, got the time and space for its revival. The well-developed occupational therapy program, that included a large component of "art therapy", became a relaxing time and space for me during the free time I had, as it provided a badly needed stress buster. I was able to encourage a number of the staff to join me in an art group, which eventually became a sort of "art club" that also included interested patients. The availability of the excellent facilities for pottery, ceramics and clay-work brought me back to what I had left behind years before in Cairo, during my "anatomy" years and my courses in art. I found it most relaxing to work with clay and use the hospital kiln to fire my sculptures and experiment with new ideas using mixed types of coloured clay. It was a most relaxing activity, and in a short time I had enough sculptures to donate as gifts and prizes for fundraising and other occasions to promote mental health. I still keep a few of my sculptures as mementos of a very interesting time (see the photos included). Meanwhile, I also took up painting again, inspired by a number of patients under my care, who happened to be professional and gifted artists. One of them in particular, AW, was a gifted and highly creative painter, whose many paintings and sketches adorned

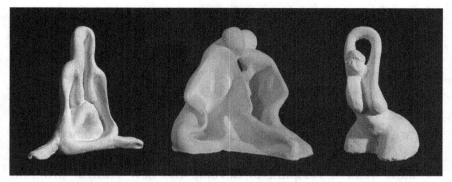

Photo of three sculptures – natural clay, each 12" tall
(by the author, A.G. Awad)

many public places, as well as being exhibited in some of the major art galleries in New York and other big cities. I recall his endless sketches during his admissions and how funny it was that he frequently caricatured and sketched me and other staff, putting his sketches under the door of my hospital office with a request for one dollar to be left for him at the nursing station (see the photo of one of his sketches).

Sketch by a patient
(Pastel on paper 24" x 36")

Not only were there gifted painters, but also occasionally we used to have talented poets and writers. I recall a young woman who had multiple admissions, suffering from psychotic episodes related to schizophrenia, as she used to copiously compose poems and kept them as a secret in her red book. Occasionally, she would request to read one of her poems in the weekly community meeting, criticizing the care she was getting, or about staff members she liked or disliked. It was only in the last week before I moved to another job, joining Toronto Western Hospital to develop the new clinical program "Medical Psychiatry", that she handed me a departing gift of a few of her poems about me. One of her memorable poems, dated 1977, not only defined her clear talents and the power of her imaginative mind, at a time when she was struggling with hearing disruptive voices and distracted by her unreal train of bizarre thoughts. A copy of one such poem, which has survived for years in my personal file, has frequently assured me in my belief about the closeness of paranoid delusional thinking to creative and imaginative thoughts (see inserted copy of the poem). Indeed, recent brain neuro-imaging studies seem to suggest the possibility of an overlap between the brain regions that control creativity and those that deal with emotions and imaginative thinking which can serve as a predisposition to a paranoid coloration of the thinking process.

```
                    Time In Rhyme

There he stood in my dream in a red devils' suit,
The point I'm trying to make is really quite moot,
But the funny thing was the copper distillery. equipment,
Maybe he was waiting for the next fallafel shipment.

I was kept under his care for one-eighth of a year,
And all his Haloperidol injections made me live in fear,
After four weeks my arms and bottom were quite sore,
And I thanked him when he finally opened the door.

I'll never forget his medical case presentation,
And it probably filled him with great joy and elation,
To show the skillful job he did of resurecting me,
And just think- it was all under OHIP- no extra fee!

But at least he's no deadbeat or any dead fish,
And when we meet in the mall we greet and we wish,
Each other well and I continue to go on my way,
I'm still quite psychotic but what's there to say?


                              September, 1977.
```

Time in Rhyme
(A poem by a patient, originally composed on a typewriter.)

I regret that art therapy and similar psychiatric treatment approaches have been mostly abandoned. Whether such approaches were overshadowed by the ease of prescribing medications or as a result of the lack of funding, the field is certainly missing an important vehicle for psychiatric healing and recovery. Enriching the subjective world of our patients can be helpful, as has been proven by a number of serious studies, or at least as Pablo Picasso once expressed it, "Art cleans the soul from the dust of everyday life".

The Thirty-Year Search for Why Patients with Schizophrenia Hated Taking Their Antipsychotic Medications

To research why the three patients with schizophrenia decided to take their lives after weeks of bitterly complaining about their medications and refusing to take them, proved to be a mystery and a significant scientific challenge. But, before I present further details, I need to define what was and still is the concept of schizophrenia.

What is Schizophrenia?

Schizophrenia is a disabling long-term psychiatric disorder that usually starts early in life and follows a chronic course, with acute episodes of exacerbation that are severe enough to require, at times, admissions to hospital. The disorder impacts several important brain functions, such as thinking, reasoning, affect and mood, cognitive abilities and overall general functioning. The disorder is heterogeneous, in terms of the broad range of symptoms that vary according to the stage of the illness. In the acute phase, the picture is dominated by frank psychotic symptoms that can include delusions, paranoid ideations, hallucinations, agitation and disturbed behaviour. Such a seriously disturbing cluster of symptoms is referred to as "positive psychotic symptoms". In the subacute and chronic states, the picture is that of deficits and "negative symptoms" that can include apathy, blunted affect and inability to experience pleasure. The person generally is withdrawn and difficult to socially engage or appropriately engage in regular tasks. Such a group of symptoms are known as "negative symptoms" or "deficit symptoms" and lead to a state of disability. Subtle or more significant "cognitive deficits" are noted throughout the long course of the illness.

Historically, in 1889, the German neurologist and well-known neuropathologist Emil Kraeplin, following lengthy clinical observations and reviews of written notes about chronic psychotic patients in mental asylums, formalized his conceptual thinking by proposing the separation of the long-term psychotic patients into two distinct groups based on their long-term outcome. The group that had a poor outcome and generally suffered from severe and deteriorated condition, were categorized as suffering from "Dementia Praecox". In contrast, the group with a more favourable outcome were mostly suffering from Manic Depressive and other serious mood disorders. A few years later, in 1908, the Swiss neurologist Eugene Bleuler refined the Kraeplinean concept and renamed the condition "Schizophrenia", instead of the original name of dementia praecox, as was proposed by Emil Kraeplin. The concept of schizophrenia, proposed by Eugene Bleuler, was the model that was adopted by most of the classificatory systems, such as the DSM and ICDU. After almost a century of extensive research, up to the present time, the etiological psycho-neuropathology of schizophrenia continues to be a mystery. A broad range of etiological factors have been considered, including concepts ranging from developmental birth brain injuries, to the discarded schizophrenogenic mothers and family schisms, to genetic defects.

With the introduction of the first specific antipsychotic and dopamine blocker, chlorpromazine, the dopamine hypothesis was introduced as an observation by Jacque Van Rossom in 1967, and eventually was refined and expanded by Professor Philip Seeman and his research team at the University of Toronto. The most confirmatory evidence by Seeman and his group was the demonstration that all antipsychotic medications could block dopamine receptors in the brain in direct relationship to their clinical potency. On the other hand, in a few years it became clinically clear that dopamine blockers, such as chlorpromazine and other similar medications, were mostly effective against the group of psychotic symptoms known as the "positive symptoms", with little or no impact on negative symptoms or cognitive deficits. Psychopathologically, recent studies indicate that the tripartite groups of symptoms; positive, negative and cognitive, though frequently associated, seem to function independently from each other, a finding that points to the likelihood of different etiological origins. Several studies, including ours, strongly point in this direction. At last, and most recently, the FDA has accepted the notion of developing medications for the treatment of a single dimension, such as a negative or a cognitive dimension, after a long time of resisting the idea. In retrospect, I believe that the broad definition of schizophrenia to include the three symptoms group, which served as the starting point for any research project, may have obscured or contributed to the frequent failure of several research projects to clarify etiological issues. It is well known that psychotic symptoms can cut across several diagnostic entities, such as dementia, delirium and drug-induced. That clearly suggests that using a dimensional approach, rather than the invalidated grouping of symptoms, may lead to clearer and better research outcomes. I do believe the concept of schizophrenia, as proposed by Kraeplin and Bleular, needs to be revisited and deconstructed, as proposed in a later chapter.

The Thirty-Year Project - Uncovering Why Some Patients with Schizophrenia Hated to Take Medications

The shocking and tragic suicide by the three patients with schizophrenia who hated and resisted taking medications, left us with a major scientific puzzle that required the development of a major scientific inquiry. Treating the project as a major scientific challenge, and prior to the development of an appropriate research design, we needed to be sure that our clinical observations were not the result of coincidence or accidentally happening, we decided to conduct a case-control retrospective chart-search of patients with the diagnosis of schizophrenia and who had committed suicide in the hospital during a ten-year period. The search yielded sixty-seven patients who had been consistently assigned the diagnosis of schizophrenia and were treated with antipsychotic medications and had committed suicide between the years of 1966 to 1976. This group was then matched with sixty-seven living patients with schizophrenia, who were treated with medications in the same hospital. Both groups were exhaustively matched for age, sex, marital status, the length of accumulated hospitalizations, and the time and type of programs in which they were treated.

A thorough analysis of the extracted data revealed no difference in the type nor the pattern of medication prescriptions in both groups, except for more extrapyramidal symptoms, such as akathisia and rigidity, as well as more subjective complaints in the suicided group. That, at least, gave us the green light to proceed. As we became concerned about the suicides and the possible link to medications, we decided to write a brief clinical report about our observations, to alert physicians regarding such tragic events. We sent our report to the Journal of Nervous and Mental Diseases, and we did not wait long before receiving a polite letter of decline to publish, accompanied by a note that the reviewers found it interesting, but considered it "soft science". As discouraging as was the characterization of soft science, we decided to move forward with a design to demonstrate that the issue was not a soft science, but rather a serious clinical challenge that required a clear understanding.

As in validation of any scientific concept, we had to meet certain requirements that included defining the concept of "subjective tolerability to medications" and outline its boundaries. To be able to do that, we had to develop reliable and psychometrically credible measurement tools, such as the "Drug Attitude Inventory" (DIA). We had to establish that patients with schizophrenia were capable of providing a reliable and consistent accountant of their inner feelings, which we demonstrated with several subjective states, such as repeated assessments of satisfaction or quality of life. Both subjective tolerability to medication and satisfaction of quality of life were typical subjective constructs. We introduced a number of conceptual psychosocial and psychobiological models to guide our research efforts. Finally, we had to document the consequences of negative subjective responses of medications and its impact on the course of the illness and its important outcomes. We did this extensive work over a number of years, which culminated in a series of publications that garnered a good deal of enthusiasm and interest in the topic. With all the collected evidence clearly pointing to the validity and clinical importance of the concept of subjective tolerability to antipsychotic medication we felt reassured. Yet, we were still unable to uncover the neurobiological basis underlying the concept, as a result of the lack of the medical technology to see what was going on inside the brain, at the neuromolecular level. It was not till the 1990s, with the advent of neuroimaging techniques, that opened a window on the internal functioning of the brain in real time.

By that time, we already had enough evidence to focus on the neurochemical, dopamine, which was known as the "pleasure molecule". The earlier observation of Jacques Van Rossum in 1967, was presented at the Fifth International Congress of the Collegium Internationale Neuropsychopharmacologiam in Amsterdam, proposing a significant role for dopamine in specific areas of the brain in the development of psychotic states. It also documented the impact of dopamine-blocking medications, such as chlorpromazine, in alleviating psychotic symptoms through the blockade of the dopamine receptors. As outlined before, the extensive work by Professor Philip Seeman and his team in Toronto, established the concept of the dopamine hypothesis as a central concept in the genesis of psychosis and its medication treatment.

By early 1990, with the availability of neuroimaging techniques, I had a clear idea that the dopamine molecule is one of the main culprits behind the development of neuroleptic-induced dysphoric states. Awaiting a bright graduate student to join our research team, and with the strong personal belief that complex and challenging research questions best be assigned to a bright doctoral student, I was happy when Dr. Lakshmi Voruganti joined me as a PhD student and I became his supervisor. At the same time, I was glad to welcome Dr. Ronald Heselgrave, a senior neuropsychologist who joined us, providing the opportunity for a capable research team to tackle the challenge of exploring the role of dopamine in the development of medication-induced dysphoric states.

Not long after assembling our team, we were able to design an experimental study to create a physiological and a neurochemical state that was equivalent to what antipsychotic medications do; block or deplete the chemical dopamine in a specific part of the brain, the nigrostriatal region at the base of the brain. To achieve this, we relied on the use of an already approved medication that was currently in use, alpha-methyl-para-tyrosine (AMPT), which depletes catecholamines and is used as an emergency treatment of the rather rare medical condition "Pheochromocytoma". The design of the study was rather complex and required the hospitalization of the participants who volunteered for the study. It also required the assembly of a large number of highly trained medical technicians to handle the neuroimaging components. The purpose of the study was to document the emerging changes in nigrostriatal dopamine functioning and observe changes in the mental state and behaviour of patients with the diagnosis of schizophrenia, who had been medication-free for at least three months, using SPECT imaging and MRI before and after dopamine depletion. An extensive number of scales were administered before dopamine depletion and for forty-eight hours afterward. Behavioural and subjective responses were tested at twelve-hour intervals. Our in-vivo study demonstrated, for the first time, the inverse relationship between striatal dopamine activity, as represented by the calculation of the D_2 receptor binding ratios, and the severity of the ensuing dysphoric responses.

Upon observing the neuropsychological and behavioural cascade of events that followed dopamine depletion in the next forty-eight hours, the patients' temporal sequence was clear and corresponded to the sequence of events in the clinical setting after ingesting an antipsychotic medication. Subjective and dysphoric response symptoms were reported as the earliest change, in less than a couple of hours, to be followed by mood and then motor symptoms, such as akathisia and muscle rigidity. Finally, cognitive changes, such as confusion and a decreased level of alertness, made their presence known. All were truly complex responses that could impact important brain functions and clearly explains how some patients had felt on the medications, and eventually ended up disliking or hating to take their medications. By all measures, it was a triumphant conclusion to a thirty-year research study that had started as a clinical observation, following the tragic death of the three patients who paid with their life to be listened to regarding their complains about medications. It underscored the value and importance of keen clinical observations at the bedside, in generating valuable research ideas, moving it to the research bench and back to the bedside. On the practical clinical side, our discovery clearly revealed the value of using a low-potency dopamine-blocking medications to avoid the development of the disturbing dysphoric responses that undermine compliance with medications and the resulting poor outcomes, as well as increasing the vulnerability to comorbid drug addiction, as will be outlined later.

An interesting incident came to light in the final phase of statistical analysis. One of the patient's dopamine results spiked in the opposite direction of the expected change. Instead of depleting dopamine content, the reverse occurred and more dopamine was released. In interviewing the patient, he confessed to smoking a joint of marijuana secretly in the washroom during a brief recess between neuroimaging sessions, and, as expected, this led to his exclusion from the analysis. On the other hand, the surreptitious incident and resulting neuroimage of marijuana releasing a flood of dopamine, proved to be the first image of such an in-vivo response. Obviously, such an image confirming the action of marijuana could not be regularly planned, since marijuana at that time was still listed in the illegal drugs schedule. This unplanned incident taught us how important it is to closely watch participants, particularly in sensitive research designs, and how a surreptitious event can be the origin of some important scientific studies. We were pleased to be the first to report such a neuroimage in the Journal of Psychiatry Research in 2006.

Meanwhile, another glitch caused the delay in the publication of our research results. We submitted our manuscript, including all the details of our neuroimaging as the first study to uncover the neurobiology of neuroleptic-induced dysphoria, to the journal Neuropsychopharmacology, then waited for few months to get the journal's decision. Finally contacting the journal, we were upset to learn that the manuscript was lost during the relocation of their editorial office from the USA to Europe. It was a regrettable incident of delay for a few months before the manuscript was eventually published in the year 2001, in "Neuropsychopharmacology". Unfortunately, science research in recent years has become a race of time in the quest of being the first to publish and own a new discovery, in a fiercely competitive research world. Nevertheless, there was delight and satisfaction in shepherding a study along for almost thirty-years and leading it to its successful conclusion, with the help and acknowledgement of several major contributions from colleagues and trainees who joined our program over the years.

Self-Medication and How Antipsychotic Medications Can Contribute to Drug Abuse

It is widely recognized that persons with schizophrenia take to substance use and abuse much more frequently than in non-psychiatric populations. Patients suffering from schizophrenia tend to seek more stimulating substances, such as heavy coffee drinking and smoking, as well as the misuse and abuse of illicit drugs. Several epidemiological studies have confirmed such a serious trend. One of the largest studies conducted was what is known as the Catchment Area Survey that included over 20,000 respondents, ages eighteen and older, conducted in three USA catchment areas between the years 1980 to 1984. Results were startling, yet not surprising for those clinicians who deal with patients suffering from schizophrenia. According to their published data, 47% of persons with schizophrenia, compared to only 13.5% of the general population, have or had evidence of drug abuse. Persons with schizophrenia have been estimated to be four to six times more likely to have drug abuse problems, than persons with no psychiatric problems, which is an alarming statistic.

There were many theories that have attempted to explain such a high frequency of comorbid drug abuse in schizophrenia and have included genetic predisposition or biochemical origins. In one hypothesis, the "self-medication hypothesis" seemed to attract attention, at least in its early years. According to this hypothesis, persons with schizophrenia take to drug use and abuse as a direct consequence of dealing with aspects of their distressing illness experiences to alleviate some of the very inconvenient effects of antipsychotic medications. Another rival hypothesis for self-medication was advanced by David F. Duncan and his colleagues about a year later, in 1974, who extensively postulated that drug abuse served as a coping mechanism against the distressing experiences of suffering from schizophrenia. In contrast, to the original hypothesis advanced by Khantzian and colleagues in 1973, which was psychoanalytically based and formulated, the Duncan hypothesis was behaviourally based and makes a clear distinction between drug use and abuse.

According to the Duncan formulation, most of those who take illicit substances do not end in dependence and only a minority of less than 20% end in abusing and becoming dependent on drugs. This very important distinction came recently to a different light, on the occasion of introducing changes related to addictive disorders in the fifth edition of the American Psychiatric Association's Diagnostic and Statistical Manual (DSM5), which abandoned the distinction between use and abuse, based on the incorrect assumption that it is difficult to ascertain the distinction between the two states. It is very unfortunate that such a crude change ended in creating far more persons who then can be deemed, according to the new DSM5 classification, to be suffering from an addiction disorder. Having in mind the wide use of illicit substances among the population and just taking the example of the heavy use of substances on various university campuses, one cannot ignore the unfortunate possible consequences of many students who can be diagnosed as suffering from addiction disorder and could probably be charged and forced to take treatments they do not need. This is just one problem, but a major one illustrating the considerable deficiencies in the psychiatric classificatory systems, as discussed in another chapter.

Getting back to our findings in neuroleptic-induced disorders, in confirmation of the thrust of the self-medication hypothesis, we conducted a survey among patients with schizophrenia attending one of our clinics. We were able to report a significant association between dysphoric responses to antipsychotic medications and drug abuse. Though we recognized that association is not a causation, the high odds ratio (4.08, $chi^2 = 21.8$, p>0.001) was rather striking and convincing. It meant that patients with schizophrenia are more susceptible to developing a vulnerability for drug abuse.

A few years later, we were fortunate to uncover the neurobiological origins of neuroleptic dysphoria related to alterations in dopamine functioning in the striatal region of the brain. Meanwhile, recent advances in the neuroscience of addiction states, confirmed the role of dopamine in the same region of the brain that is responsible for the vulnerability of patients with schizophrenia to drug addiction. We finally were fortunately able to propose a neurobiologically-based hypothesis, by connecting the dots between neuroleptic-induced dysphoria and a vulnerability to addictive disorders. This immediately clarified why patients with schizophrenia and comorbid abuse never benefited from the use of antipsychotic medication that had a strong dopamine-blocking effect, such as chlorpromazine or haloperidol. In fact, by using such a medication, as we did for years, unwittingly worsened the addiction component. I cannot recall using either medication in the early era of not having an alternative, that any of the patients I treated gave up abusing substances while on chlorpromazine or similar medications.

Looking back almost thirty years ago, when we developed our program of subjective tolerability to medications and all the effort that went into making the program such a success, it certainly affirmed the value of clinical observations in creating clinical research studies, from the bedside to the research bench and back to the bedside. It once more highlights the advice made centuries ago by the ancient Swiss physician and medical scientist Paracelsus, who advocated the important value of systematic and astute clinical observations in advancing the science of medicine. I will always be grateful to the many persons who worked extensively with me in developing and maintaining a thirty-year program; Tom Hogan, Lakshmi Voruganti and Ron Heselgrave, and the many trainees who joined the program as part of their training. Above all, my due respect goes to the three patients who tragically paid with their lives, to be listened to regarding their complaints about medications.

As a follow-up action, after establishing the possible link between comorbid drug vulnerability and neuroleptic-induced dysphoric responses, in a published report in 2015 we raised the issue of whether it is time to re-examine the process of the development of new antipsychotic medications, by establishing comorbid substance abuse as a new clinical indication for the development of new antipsychotic medication. I do believe that the issue of comorbid addictions and the field of addictions itself, will continue as a major focus of neuroscience research efforts. There is a rising momentum at present for the clear understanding of the full neurobiology of addictive states. The addition to the literature of addictions has been recently enriched by Professor Victor R. Preedy from King's College in London, UK, in his definitive three volumes of Neuropathology of Drug Addictions and Substance Misuse (2016), to which he was kind to ask me to provide a chapter, that is included in Volume 1: The Neurobiology of Comorbid Addictions in Psychiatric Disorders. The book, in its extensive three volumes, will serve as the most inclusive reference text book for years to come, as well as an informative guide for both researchers, clinicians and policy makers.

Can New Drug Development be Left for Market Forces? The Development of the International Society for Central Nervous System (CNS) Clinical Trials Methodology (ISCTM)

The discovery and the introduction of the first specific antipsychotic medication chlorpromazine in the early 1950s, ushered in a period of therapeutic optimism and great expectations for psychiatric new drug developments, which lasted for about a decade. As the only new medications that followed were just copies of chlorpromazine with slight tweaks here and there, including all the new me-too medications that shared the same serious side-effects, a period of stagnation followed. An era of serious concern dawned on the field of new drug developments, particularly given that several of the clinical trials of new psychiatric medications had failed. Many serious questions arose regarding the adequacy and appropriateness of clinical trials methodology, as well as the central question of whether the development of new psychiatric medications could be entirely left to market forces. Meanwhile, the field of schizophrenia, both clinically and academically, was gaining more interest and momentum. The rising expectations and the need for an international forum to provide a platform for clinicians and researchers to present their work and their thoughts about schizophrenia was seized in the mid-1980s by two UK professors, Tim Crow and Steven Hirsch, who organized what became known as the "Biennial Schizophrenia Workshop". The meeting was to convene every second year in the month of February, in the city of Davos, Switzerland, following the annual meeting there of the International Economic Forum. The idea behind this arrangement was simply an opportunity for a family ski vacation, to add to the science. The plan quickly caught on, as the meeting became the highlight of a pleasant exchange of ideas and the development of an international collaboration.

I was fortunate to attend and participate in the very successful biennial meetings, frequently forging small group discussions about specific issues and scientific challenges. For a number of years my ongoing discussions with my colleague, Dr. Ravi Anand, about the problems and stagnation in the development of better psychiatric medications, continued from one meeting to the next. It was not until the meeting of February 2004, that both of us concluded our biennial discussions about the urgent need to develop an international platform for dealing with the challenges of central nervous system medications and their clinical trials methodology. We both had a rough idea that to achieve such a plan it would need to be an international multidisciplinary forum, public and not-for-profit, and to be partnered with academia, the pharmaceutical industry, regulatory agencies and the public. Having Ravi as a senior member of the pharmaceutical industry, and very knowledgeable about the international scene of pharmaceutical developments, proved to be extremely helpful. The plan was immediately put into action. Soon Ravi connected me with a few senior colleagues who shared the same ideas and concerns. As a follow-up, after numerous and lengthy conference calls, a meeting was organized to take place in Toronto in September 2004, and included a few colleagues as founders, Larry Alphs, George Gharabawi, Richard Hartman, Mark Rapaport, Steven Potkin, Ravi Anand and myself.

There we were, early in September 2004, meeting in my office at Humber River Hospital in Toronto, a University of Toronto affiliated hospital, but we missed Mark Rapaport and Steven Potkin, as they were unable to attend. The early decision of the meeting was to continue discussions until we reached a consensus about the plan that included the goals and objectives, a charter and a plan for action. By the end of two days of lengthy discussions a consensus was reached on the development of the "International Society for CNS Clinical Trials and Methodology", with goals to serve as a forum to re-evaluate current concepts of CNS drug development, including new medications, trials methodology, associated guidelines, modes of usage of these drugs, and the clinical methodology used both in research and practice. Another major goal was to address and manage the potential conflicts between research objectives/ indications, regulatory demands/requirements, and the drug class/ indication and clinical feasibility in the CNS area. To achieve these goals the ISCTM should engage in critically reviewing and analyzing issues related to the design and conduct of CNS clinical trials, both failed and successful, and debate current controversies in CNS trials methodology. ISCTM also had to discuss gaps between regulatory requirements and clinical developments, and improve the interpretation of clinical data for regulators and prescribers. As well, ISCTM was to review the potential impact of new medical technologies in clinical trials, including ethical and legal issues, by the development of position statements on current issues in CNS clinical research. In spite of the short timeline, it was enthusiastically decided to hold the first annual meeting the following year, on February 22 - 24, 2005, in Montreal, Canada. Tasks were quickly defined and Larry Alphs was asked to take the responsibility for the preparation of the first annual meeting. I recall how everyone left Toronto with great enthusiasm and hope of making such a challenging and badly needed project become successful in its impact on the process of development of new CNS medications.

The period between September 2004 and February 22, 2005, proved to be a hive of activities in laying down the basics of the new society. Dr. Oakley Ray and his management company in Nashville was recruited to provide the administrative and management structure, based on his expertise in managing the annual meeting of the American College of Neuropsychopharmacology. This meant that the first home for the society was also to be located in Nashville, Tennessee. A number of prominent neuroscientists, psychiatrists and neurologists were contacted as potential members or speakers for the annual meeting. The enthusiasm we encountered facilitated our task. It felt like we had hit the right time, that many in the field had been waiting for. Tasks were assigned for raising supporting funds, but with the clear proviso of no marketing to be allowed. Recruiting members was the essence of ascertaining balance in membership, realizing in advance that there would be more membership from pharmaceutical industry, recognizing the sheer size of it. To offset this potential and not be seen as an appendix to the pervasive interest of the pharmaceutical industry, emphasis was given to the recruitment of academic members, noting in advance the tension between academia and the industry, and the tendency of both academia and the pharmaceutical industry to operate independently.

Having members from regulatory agencies proved to be rather difficult, at least initially. While members from various regulatory agencies were permitted to become members as individuals, the regulatory agencies, as a government entity, were not allowed by government rules to become formal partners, though they could respond to invitations to participate in scientific meetings. It took some time for me to understand the reasoning behind such strict FDA rules, which were meant to dispel any suspicion of bias or impropriety in the conduct of approval and licensing of new products. Obviously, they had learned lessons from negative experiences in the past. One of the interesting situations that I encountered quickly, after I began serving as the first Founding President of ISCTM, was to make a presentation on behalf of ISCTM to one of the FDA expert panels, related to the long-term effects of medications and its impact on clinical trials design. Two members of the FDA panel surprisingly turned out to be past students of mine, who had joined me for part of their training. What took me by surprise was that they were strictly instructed not to contact or interact with external presenters representing third parties. Initially, I was baffled by how they uncomfortably tried to distance themselves and avoided talking to me during a coffee recess. At first, I thought that if the FDA could not trust their own invited experts, then there was something wrong. On the other hand, I quickly realized the need, not only for independence, but also the appearance of being independent. This particular issue became vivid in my memory again many years later, in 2019-2020, when composing this chapter at a time when the highest political officials in the USA were making every crooked effort to subvert and influence decisions by the FDA, to suit their misplaced political ambitions. Now I clearly understand why regulatory agencies need to fiercely defend their independence and neutrality, and the need for the public and professionals to support their independence.

Getting back to the ISCTM's inaugural meeting in Montreal, surprisingly, in spite of the short notice, over 130 meeting registrants began to arrive, during one of the serious snow storms that Montreal is known for. The high attendance of the first meeting of a society that had only existed for a few months was a pleasant surprise, but also provided us with reassurance and a clear confirmation that we were heading in the right direction at the right moment in time. The program was strong and the speakers covered important topics that included issues such as establishing long-term efficacy, the impact of attrition on outcome, the use of biological markers as end points, mild cognitive impairment as an indication and many other topics, including a data blitz session. Different from other meetings, every presentation was followed by an equal amount of time for comments and discussions. One of the innovative additions to the program was the inclusion of "round table" discussions that included inviting scientific journal editors, radio and print journalists, to discuss publications of study results, negative or failed – "damned if you do and damned if you can't". Suffice to say, the two days of the inaugural meeting were a great success, and was influential in the recruitment of new members.

The business meeting, the first for ISCTM, provided a very important endorsement and support. The first formal founding of the executive committee was voted in, which included Ravi Anand (Treasurer), Larry Alphs (Program Committee), A. George Awad (President), Ross Baldessarini (Scientific Committee), George Gharabawi (Membership), Richard Hartman (Secretary), Steven Potkin (Scientific Committee) and Mark Rapaport (Scientific Committee). The founding members who played major roles in the consultations leading up to the founding of ISCTM included Munaf Ali, Roger Bullock, Dilip Jeste, Ranga Krishnan, Ramy Mahmoud, Atul Pande and Scott Reines. The annual business meeting also confirmed Oakley Ray as ISCTM's Coordinator.

Then the hard work began, to cautiously attract new members, not to build ISCTM into a big and unmanageable organization, but to invite and select members who could make a scientific contribution. Fulfilling its mandate, the ISCTM annual meeting proved to be a diverse menu of high science and its application. The significant approval and success of the annual meeting led to the addition of a summer meeting that frequently focused on a single important issue, sometimes working with other societies in or out of the USA. The addition of a "National Mental Health Research to Policy Forum" attracted a good number of experts in mental health research and policy making. Joining forces in some meetings with other scientific agencies that deal with CNS issues broadened the base and allowed for further collaborative efforts. Mentoring young investigators attracted a number of aspiring candidates, who by now had become senior investigators in their own right and expertise. With the passing away of Dr. Oakley Ray, his assistant, the very capable Ms. Carlotta McKee, assumed the Executive Director role of the flourishing and rapidly growing ISCTM. Overall, looking back fifteen years, the ISCTM continues its progress from being just an idea that took several years to hatch, to becoming a credible and strong forum and platform for its members, representing academia, the pharmaceutical industry, regulatory agencies and the public, to meet face to face and unencumbered by barriers or self-interest.

I am particularly delighted that some of the concerns that I had worried about during the early years of my presidency, did not materialize. One concern was the survival of the organization and whether the initial enthusiasm and support would be sustained. Another major concern was based on my extensive experiences in other national and international scientific and professional organizations, and how to avoid the pitfalls that ruined some of those organizations. Adhering to strict democratic rules, while respecting openness and transparency has saved ISCTM from giving way to the interest of one group taking over, or the perception of a "big brother" monopoly. Maintaining a balance was a priority, in spite of the size and influence of the large group representing the interests of the pharmaceutical industry in dominating the society, fortunately did not happen, to their credit. It is not that ISCTM had a largely smooth free ride. Since tensions have always been part of the growing pains of any diverse organization, what mattered was how to transparently resolve tensions and mend cracks. I am proud and optimistic about the success of the ISCTM project, that was sustained by the contribution of its founders and all its active members. My hope that its progress and impact will continue, and that it adheres to its charter and preserves its independent course.

Though I am writing this chapter about events of the recent past, I could not free myself from worrying about events of the recent present, which is the reprehensible and vicious attempts by the highest office in the US to corrupt the FDA process of licensing drugs and vaccines. The persistent and coercive attempts to do so, in the face of admirable resistance by the FDA and its director, is worth noting, not only to compliment the FDA for taking a stand, but also as an alarm bell for the need to strengthen regulatory agencies in their pursuit of independence to conduct the process of approval of new drugs scientifically and without the fear of pressure and bias. For that to happen, agencies like the FDA have to continuously review their progress in updating their requirements and rules, to meet the test of time.

The Pharmaceutical Industry and New Drug Development - Developing New Medications is Complex, Lengthy and Expensive

In returning back to the question of whether new drug development can be left to market forces, collectively, it was estimated a few years ago that the top twenty pharmaceutical companies spent about $60 billion annually on research and drug development. The average cost of bringing a new drug to market, including drug failures, was about $2.6 billion, with a range between $765.9 million to $2.7716 billion, depending on the clinical targets and the process details. Generally, drug development in certain clinical areas, such as immunology and oncology, tend to be more expensive. Spreading the expense of failures tends to further inflate the cost, which, altogether, adds to the high price of drugs for patients.

The process of new drug development is rather complex and can take years, barring the many and frequent failures at various stages. The early preclinical phase involves a laborious screening for molecules or compounds that may have the potential for clinical development. It is estimated that 5000 – 10,000 molecules need to be searched, to identify ten to twenty potential candidates. In recent years, such a laborious process has been facilitated by the presence of several big data sets and the availability of powerful computers and artificial intelligence (AI) approaches. Potential candidates are then subjected to animal pharmacology and toxicology, followed by an application for Investigational New Drug (IND) program approval, to conduct clinical pharmacology studies in healthy volunteers. Early therapeutic studies in small scale trials are then followed by main therapeutic studies in large scale clinical studies on representative patient groups. This is the critical phase for establishing efficacy, effectiveness, appropriate dosing and side effects profile. This is the phase that is critical, in terms of design, the population recruited, choosing investigators and the countries included, as well as appropriate monitoring and quality control. Post-marketing studies frequently follow approval by regulatory bodies.

In summary, it is a lengthy process that not only requires extensive financial investment, but also a high level of expertise in a wide range of scientific fields. It's no wonder that the critical development process and, particularly, the main multi-centre clinical studies are frequently referred to as "the big bang" or "black hole", with success to be guaranteed only at the very tail end. Sometimes success or failure have to wait until the product has been already marketed and in use. In my long career of association with several new psychiatric medication developments, I was part of two very promising medications; Zimelidine, which would have been the first Serotonin-specific antidepressant, but was pulled out of use shortly after its introduction, as a result of serious side-effects that had not been observed during the lengthy trial phases. The other medication was the antipsychotic Remoxipride, that would have been the first of the new class of atypical antipsychotics, except for the unexpected serious side effects that emerged in the post-marketing phase. In fact, the main therapeutic pivotal studies were conducted in Canada, and neither I nor others could recall noticing any signs that pointed to such serious side-effects that followed use in the general population.

Overall, in spite of the many and sometimes harsh and warranted criticism of the pharmaceutical industry, in terms of their marketing approaches and lack of transparency, particularly with regard to failed clinical trials and hiding potential serious side-effects, such as addiction in the case of opioids, by and large the majority of the big pharmaceutical companies did a reasonable job. After all, pharmaceutical companies are not non-profit entities. A series of important reforms were introduced by the major pharmaceutical firms to meet some of the public concerns, such as more openness, transparency and serious collaborative attitudes. The high cost of drug development and its annual escalation has been forcing the pharmaceutical industry to reform the process of new drug development, by using the new electronic technologies and streamlining methodologies to shorten the timeline from preclinical studies to approval or failure.

I strongly believe that a much closer collaboration between academia and the pharmaceutical industry could be helpful and would provide an economy of resources and time. But, then, I do not believe in leaving the process of new drug development completely or entirely to market forces. A good example of this is how to deal with the development and the flood of the me-too drugs, when the market is already saturated. Obviously, any well-run pharmaceutical company will likely hesitate before introducing another me-too drug, simply for lack of profitability and a waste of energy and resources. Yet, there needs to be strict formal requirements, such as the FDA should not grant IND approval for me-too applications, unless the drug provides documented additional benefits or presents a new advance in formulation or technology. I believe that the market forces can exert a powerful, competitive impact, but within a set of clear, fair and practical rules and requirements that include a shorter patent life or an earlier introduction of generics. In that context, academia and other scientific independent organizations, such as ISCTM, can produce regular scientific position papers that can guide and influence scientific thinking within the pharmaceutical industry and their decision makers. The bottom line, at present, is to not only enhance the process of discovery in producing new, more effective and safe medications, but also to reduce the escalating costs of new medications for patients, and making them more accessible. There is no value in developing better medications, if patients cannot afford them.

PART VII

Quality of Care in Psychiatry

Quality – What Is Quality?

Over the past several decades, the term "quality" has been extensively used as an attribute to a wide range of objects and transactions, including health care services and, by extension, psychiatric care. It is not difficult to recognize what is meant by *quality shoes* or a *quality* menu in a restaurant. On the other hand, it is more difficult to define what is meant by the quality of a piece of music or, for that matter, to describe what is the quality of health care services. Yet, "quality" as a term, has been attached to a long list of important health concepts, such as quality of care, quality review, quality improvements, quality assurance, quality of life, and the list goes on. What, then, is quality? It is certainly becoming almost meaningless if we cannot define it. Reflecting on such a quandary, several years ago, Robert M. Pirsig, described "quality" in his classic book, "Zen and the Art of Motorcycle Maintenance", like this: "Quality... you know what it is, yet you do not know what it is... Some things are better than others, that is, they have more quality... But when you try to say what quality is... there is nothing to talk about... if no one knows what it is, then for all practical purposes, it does not exist... so round and round you go, spinning mental wheels and nowhere finding any place to get traction... What the hell is quality?" That was nearly fifty years ago and at that time also applied to the state of *quality* in health care reviews. Since then, a good deal of progress has been accomplished by introducing operational definitions and exploring the conceptual models underpinning such concepts. A key factor in the development of such a broad array of concepts has been the need for a development of standards to be applied in systematic care reviews, including peer reviews, that recognize its limitations, in terms of its subjectivity, randomness and irreproducibility.

It is interesting that as early as 1933, the fundamentals of good medical care were defined in the Lee/Jones Report, from the University of Chicago, that included conceptual aspects such as acceptability, accessibility, availability, compliance, comprehensiveness, coordination, effectiveness and efficiency, however, it took years to incorporate them in care reviews. Unfortunately, such important dimensions proved of little use until the development of clear operational definitions that lead to the development of objective and reliable measurement tools.

One of the challenges in the assessment of the quality of health care and, in particular, psychiatric care, has been that we have not defined our actual and final product. For a long time, psychiatric symptom-improvement in major psychiatric disorders had been considered the main outcome of treatment, since there is no cure yet available for such conditions. But, improvement in symptoms, alone, does not mean it is the only important principle, while the person continues to be unable to go to work, becomes functional and able to enjoy life. In other words, disabilities and their negative sequences continue to represent "illness behaviour". Psychiatrists have to clearly recognize that their role, at least until now, is not as illness "curers", but more so as illness "healers". Such a distinction complicates the process of the development of appropriate standards of care and defining practical and achievable outcomes. This does not mean lowering the standards, but rather that special efforts need to be directed towards dealing with illness behaviour and minimizing disabilities. It is critical, for the proper design and planning of rehabilitation and disability financial compensation schemes, to be linked and coordinated with the need for the maintenance of continued engagement and functionality across a broad range of dimensions and outcomes. In other words, psychiatric outcomes need to be broadened beyond the improvement of symptoms, to include issues such as quality of life, wellness and the ability to function across multiple roles, both social and vocational, which will be discussed later.

PSRO – The US Health Care Initiative that Died in Partisan Ideology and Commercial Opportunism

In October 1972, Public Law 92-603 was approved by the US Congress and enacted into law. It required the establishment of the Professional Standards Review Organization (PSRO), and defined its objectives as "determining the necessity, appropriateness, and quality of medical care provided beneficiaries of the major programs authorized in the Social Security Act". As such, the PSRO hospital review system was based on three separate, but interrelated, review mechanisms; *concurrent review,* that includes admission certification and continued stay review through discharge; *medical care evaluation studies* and analysis of hospital practitioners, and patient *profile analysis.* The main reason behind the enaction of such a complex process was the attempt to contain the escalating health costs of health care services paid through Medicare, Medicaid and Maternal and Child Health programs.

Explicitly, the PSRO was to monitor services provided and deem them as medically necessary, meet professional standards, and ensure services were provided in the most economic and medically appropriate health care agencies. Each PSRO organization was required to service a specific geographical area and select or develop its own norms of care, diagnosis and treatment. In simple terms, though the PSRO law included several lofty objectives, such as quality of care standards, concurrent monitoring and reviews, it became quickly clear that for any hospital to be compensated for services provided, they had to produce enormous and extensive paperwork documentation that likely offset much of any savings.

It is very interesting that such a complex and expensive system was implemented nationwide in the US without the benefit of a limited field trial in one or two states, to test its feasibility, practicality and cost benefit. By the mid-1970s, the burden of hospitals and care providers was extensive. Here is where the genius of US capitalism came in. To ease the burden of documentation, hundreds and hundreds of management companies were established, and descended on hospitals to take care of this complex task. It was a clever commercial opportunity, but in reality it denied the chance for hospitals to take a close look inward regarding the care they were providing. The opportunity for medical staff to implement peer review or partake in the development of standards or the methods of care review vanished.

Meanwhile, as the PSRO process disintegrated into a complex paper exercise, the Congress had some second thoughts. Concerns were raised from both the left and right political factions, ranging from concerns about the rigour of the review process in physician-based organizations, to questions raised about how the program represented a serious intrusion into medical practice. The fierce debate carried on until the Reagan era in the 1980s, when it was decided to end the program, as the final outcome of intense partisan fights and massive lobbying by the management companies. On the positive side of the ledger of such a failed national experiment, was the heightened focus on quality of care and the development of an extensive and complex methodology for quality of care evaluation. Which returns me back to Canada and, specifically, to 999 Queen Street in 1978, almost two years after I joined the hospital.

Evaluation of Quality of Care in Psychiatry

A Conference, June 22, 1979, at the Queen Street Mental Health Centre

As would sometimes happen, any major developments or trends in the US, whether political or otherwise, would drift across the northern border of the US to Canada, including the PSRO debate. Though the health care systems in the US and Canada were fundamentally different, the same concerns about quality and cost of health care were equally high on the Canadian political agenda. Health care in Canada became universal in the mid-1960s, covered by tax payers, and included the right of every Canadian citizen to have reasonable access to health care. The US health care system was mostly private and entrepreneurial, except for Medicare and Medicaid, which were covered by the government and served special populations that included the poor and the elderly. Politically, in the province of Ontario, the new Conservative government of Premier Bill Davis was in power, and included the appointment of a young progressive and fiscally conservative Minister of Health, the Honourable Dennis Timbrell.

The Ministry of Health was the largest portfolio in government and in budget, but the forced increase in the costs of health care provision, related to the major advances and introduction of expensive new medical technologies, the rapid growth of big pharma and the rising demands of quality care, the new Minister of Health quickly had to face the same pressures that led to the introduction of the PSRO system in the US. It came as no surprise, then, that political rumours indicated the evolving interest of the new Health Minister in developing a PSRO-type of program, mainly for cost containment, by rationalizing quality and cost of health care, which included psychiatry. Fortunately for Canada, by 1977-1978 the many serious problems encountered in the US during the implementation of the PSRO had started to become known, through the published scientific reports and the critical comments by politicians and health care providers. Professionally, the rising concerns and fears about the provincial government going ahead with some hybrid of the failing PSRO system in the US, became a major concern for those who were closely following the PSRO developments in the US, including myself.

Then an intuitive idea flashed in my mind; what about organizing a conference or a full day symposium to include experts from both sides of the Canada/USA border, to address the issues of quality and cost of psychiatric services? I felt that it would be important to invite politicians and members of the public who were concerned about health care issues. I mulled over the idea, and in a few days I was even more convinced of the value of organizing such a conference, particularly as it felt the time was right for it. I then shared my idea with two key allies; Professor Henry Durost, the Medical Director of 999 Queen Street, and Professor Bill McCormick, Director of Continuing Medical Education for the University of Toronto and Director of Education at the 999 Queen Street psychiatric hospital. The idea was received enthusiastically, and immediately I had an organizing committee of the three of us.

The next few weeks clarified ideas and suggestions for topics and speakers, half of them to be experts from the US, and the rest were Canadian health care and academic experts. Professor Frederick Lowy, the Chair of the University of Toronto's Department of Psychiatry and the incoming Dean of the Faculty of Medicine, kindly agreed to chair the meeting. An invitation to open the conference was sent to the Honourable Dennis Timbrell, the Minister of Health, and was not only enthusiastically accepted, but he also promised help in funding the costs towards the organization of the meeting, as well as supporting the publication of the conference proceedings. Contacting the potential speakers proved to be much easier than what I had expected, likely due to the prominence of the issues belying the focus of the meeting and its current relevance. Within a few weeks we had already put together a proposal for the program, that was structured to include ample time for discussions after each presentation, and at the end of the day a general discussion that included the speakers and the audience was allotted two hours.

From the US, we were fortunate to secure the participation of three major speakers: Professor William Fifer, a senior investigator at Health Services Research Centre; Professor Richard Dorsey, from the Department of Medicine and Public Health at the University of Minneapolis, Minnesota and Chief of Psychiatry at Otto C. Epp Memorial Hospital in Cincinnati, Ohio, as well as Chairman of the APA Task Force on Psychopharmacological Criteria Development and consultant to the APA Task Force on Peer Review; Professor George Stricker, who was Chairman of the National Advisory Panel, CHAMPUS/American Psychological Association Peer Review Project.

From Canada, the speakers included: Professor Alex Richman, National Health Scientist and Professor of Psychiatry, Director of the Training and Research Unit in Psychiatric Epidemiology at Dalhousie University, Dalhousie, Nova Scotia; Professor John Sibley, Department of Medicine and Clinical Epidemiology and Biostatistics at McMaster University, Hamilton, Ontario; Professor M. G. G. Thompson, Department of Psychiatry, University of Toronto and Executive Director, Chief of Staff, West End Creche, Child and Family Clinic, Toronto, Ontario; Professor Barry Willer a Canadian working in the US, at the Division of Community Psychiatry, New York State University at Buffalo, New York, as well as Professors Durost, McCormick, Lowy and myself.

On June 22, 1979, the conference got underway with an opening statement from the Honourable Dennis Timbrell and the Chairman, Professor Frederick Lowy. The conference was well attended and included an extensive discussion after each presentation, with the general discussion at the end of the day being lively and included a wide range of related topics.

At the end of the day, after about nine hours of presentations and extensive discussions, a number of issues seemed to garner a good level of consensus. There was almost a full agreement about the value and need for ongoing health care evaluations, but not along the line of the PSRO. The development of evaluative criteria, by itself, could be a good learning process, more conducive to suit the local setting and ensure more consensus among the professionals being consulted and involved in the process. One of the interesting issues that evolved in discussions was the core difference between the American and the Canadian health care systems was the value attached to health care, in terms of the entrenchment of health care in an individual's Bill of Rights in Canada. In contrast to the US, the right of every citizen in Canada to have reasonable access to health care, including psychiatric care, was deemed the right of every citizen. Guaranteeing the right to health care also empowers patients for some responsibility, more than just being consumers of health care services.

Politically, the conference achieved one of its unspoken, but urgent, goals. At the end of the day, the Honourable Dennis Timbrell left the conference having second thoughts about his interest in developing a PSRO-like program in Ontario. At the time, though the change of mind of the Minister was perceived as a success, which it was, in the long run it yielded mixed results in leaving health care professionals and their organizations to form the design and implementation of their continued professional development and assurance of professional competence, as will be be discussed later.

The Rise of Interest in Quality of Care Assessments and Peer Reviews, But with a Questionably Low Impact

As the proceedings of the 1979 Toronto conference were published by Pergamon Press in 1980, in the book *Evaluation of Quality of Care in Psychiatry*, the themes that evolved in the presentations and discussions gained wide circulation. All attendees of the conference received a free copy of the book, and so did a large number of targeted politicians and health experts. It was clear that we managed to ward off any attempts by government to introduce heavy-handed regulations, but instead we opened the door for a more collaborative approach and a serious dialogue with professionals. Now the ball was in the court of the professional and health regulatory agencies, who were under considerable pressure to do something to assure the public of the quality of the care provided and the clinical competence of health care providers. Through extensive discussions and consultations with professional groups, it became clear that physicians, in general, would welcome self-regulation, but not much more. Physicians, on the whole, are generally highly motivated individuals who value and fiercely guard their independence. Obviously, physicians also wield considerable power as drivers of health care and costs.

On the face of such serious resistance, the professional and regulatory agencies caved in, and instead of taking the time to introduce serious conceptually and scientifically based approaches, they opted for a much softer and somewhat questionable self-directed approach. As we noted in the introduction of our book "Evaluation of Quality of Care in Psychiatry", "...it cannot be assumed that this (attending a conference or reading a book) will enhance the quality of care, unless altered treatment approaches can be demonstrated after the educational experiences", and that continues to be the crux of the main limitations of the current peer review approaches and maintenance of competency programs. There is yet no reliable and convincing evidence to prove the effectiveness or the value of the ongoing fiddly approaches, counting papers read or conferences attended, in improving clinical performance. In Canada, a more serious approach, such as re-certification every eight to ten years, that has been adopted in the US and several European countries, failed to gain traction, as a result of serious opposition.

I do admit that there is no perfect system available yet, that is based on clear, conceptually validated testing. On the other hand, by shutting the door and adopting clearly ineffective approaches seemed to undermine every effort for the continued search for better approaches that could prove to be more effective, and less costly. Quoting from a commentary in the Lancet made several years ago by the then professor of surgery at Cambridge University, "...it is anomalous that the day a man ceases to be a senior registrar on his appointment as a consultant marks the beginning of a period, extending to retirement age, in which professional criticism from his colleagues is most unlikely unless his practice is so blatant to involve a suit for damage. Yet a surgeon may spend his whole life making poor judgment...but remains unaware that his work is below par". Sure enough, these sober remarks about surgeons apply to all medical specialists, including psychiatry.

In 1979, we reported our three-year experience of conducting psychiatric audits that targeted issues identified as gaps or deficits and which resulted in a noticeable quality improvements, by adopting a corrective responses. As we were impressed by the results of the audits and its value for the professional staff who participated in its conduction and the follow-up of corrective actions, we decided to conduct a survey across the province of Ontario to establish how many hospitals had a formal process for psychiatric audits. To our surprise, only fifty percent of psychiatric hospitals and departments of psychiatry in general hospitals had any process for psychiatric audits, and more audit activities were reported in psychiatric hospitals compared to the general hospitals' departments of psychiatry. However, only one third of those who conducted audits felt it to be helpful in improving the quality of care and a useful educational experience.

Similarly, in 1991 we conducted a survey regarding the quality of psychopharmacology teaching in academic departments across Canada. The survey was motivated by a similar study published earlier, in 1979, by professor Paul Garfinkel and colleagues, that reported several deficiencies in the training of psychopharmacology across Canada. Though a number of recommendations were made and a few were implemented, such as the development of special office for psychopharmacology training, as well as research and its integration with other treatment modalities, not very much progress was accomplished. Those who, like myself, provided hospital and community consultation, failed to notice a significant improvement in the rational use of psychopharmacological agents. Part of the difficulties at that time was the reliance on the pharmaceutical companies to provide continued education in the use of psychopharmacological agents, as well as the lack of several teachers and supervisors with expertise in the field. A significant contributing factor, we found, goes back much earlier, to the interviews for the selection of candidates for psychiatric training and the preponderance of selected residents who have little interest in psychobiology, being more interested in psychotherapy and psychodynamic psychiatry. In our published report in 1991, in the Canadian Journal of Psychiatry, we observed that among ten academic post-graduate training programs in psychiatry across Canada, we continued to find many gaps and deficits that undermined appropriate training in psychopharmacology. Among the gaps we reported were inadequate training in basic psychopharmacology and a lack of its integration in the total treatment plans. Only very few academic programs provided training on how to develop or participate in a clinical trial of medications, or how to critically read and evaluate research findings and publications.

One of the remedies we undertook in Ontario, was the arrangement of periodic tours by myself and Professor Russell Joffe, to provide continued education in psychopharmacology by visiting and consulting various medical communities outside large academic centres. Unfortunately, such a model seemed to be brief in its impact, and without a regular periodic follow-up booster that the system could not support its cost, there was a noticeably slow regression back to old habits. Apart from the issue of cost, another fundamental deficiency in achieving a more significant impact in the continuing education program, is the lack of an appropriate theory or conceptual model on how to induce changes in clinical performance. In recent years, there has been evolving literature that points to the insufficiency of reliance on self-assessments, and the inadequacy of simple efforts to redress its limitations, as being the pathway to an improved clinical performance, unless it is accompanied by cognitive changes. It is very interesting that the issues and concerns of how to influence physicians' behaviour have been with us for a long time.

One of the interesting experiments that I still recall from the 1970s, was how long a refresher course for a specific medical issue would last without a booster to follow later. A group of general practitioners were invited to receive refresher training at a university academic centre, for improving their clinical skills in auscultation. A year later, without a further follow-up booster, many of them returned back to their old pattern of performance. I believe that many continuing education programs, as well as peer reviews and maintenance of competence programs, have become no more than a paper exercise, lacking any reliable proof for its effectiveness.

I am frequently being amazed at how pharmaceutical companies' marketing personnel have been more successful in their individual visits to physicians. Apart from leaving a pen or a writing pad, they've been able to persuade many physicians to prescribe their medication. Our study, as well as those of many others, have clearly demonstrated a rise of specific medication prescriptions following the visits of pharmaceutical representatives, that can last for a long time after the visit. I believe there is a lesson there on how continuing education can be successfully organized. In the end, I feel that medical education programs require ongoing reviews and updating. Unfortunately, as the knowledge itself can become quickly obsolete, as a result of the rapid acquisition of new knowledge these days, the most important and more durable skill is how to teach physicians to critically read and evaluate new knowledge and research findings, and be able to translate and incorporate new knowledge in their own practices.

As for current peer reviews and maintenance of competence programs, I believe, as discussed before, that many of them are not effective and there is no valid documentations that demonstrate its impact on improved clinical performance. I think that many of them are wasted efforts in falsely attempting to assure the public that something has been done towards improvement of clinical care. I also believe that some of the energy and funds invested, and mostly wasted there, can be redirected towards a more serious research effort on how to develop more effective continued medical education programs that are also attractive to the physicians themselves, in terms of self-interest.

PART VIII

Psychiatric Outcomes

Broadening Psychiatric Outcomes Beyond Symptom Improvement

Historically, both clinically and in clinical trials of new psychiatric medications, outcomes to psychiatric treatments have been based largely on symptom improvements. Until recently, clinical trials of new medications have seldom included other important measures, such as satisfaction, social functioning or subjective tolerability outcomes. Over the past few decades there has been increasing pressure and more interest, not only in broadening outcomes to psychiatric treatments, but also in including patients' self-reports about the management of their illness. Among the reasons for such a rising interest, is the increasing pressure by the consumers' movement in demanding that patients and their families have a more meaningful share in the clinical decision-making process, with clear expectations of better therapies and much improved outcomes. Patients as consumers of services, their views, attitudes towards health and illness, as well as their level of satisfaction of care, are becoming increasingly recognized. It has become clear that including patients in the decision-making process of the management of their psychiatric illnesses also broadens both the "outcome" dimensions and the concept of "recovery", by empowering patients to be active participants and share in the responsibility of their own improvement. It underscores the notion that psychiatric outcomes are more than symptom improvement, but also include improvement in the functional and social spheres.

The recent proliferation of reliable psychiatric assessment tools, by and large, have facilitated a shift in such emphasis toward broader outcomes. But, at the same time, and as we have frequently cautioned, reliance on psychiatric assessment tools is not a substitute for acquiring sound clinical skills. It can sometimes merely introduce a good deal of background noise by misinterpretations or inappropriate use, particularly when it comes to the timing of the assessment of certain outcomes, with the stage and course of the illness. For that, we developed a framework of appropriate assessment timing – suitable for capturing the changes of symptoms expected across the long term course of treatment.

Such a long course includes the acute or proximal phase, when the focus and expectations need to deal with managing the acute symptoms, and dealing with medication side-effects. The intermediate sub-acute phase continues to deal with emerging symptoms and side-effects, plus ascertaining medication compliance and the provision of psycho- and socio-therapies. In the distal phase, real rehabilitative therapies can be augmented and issues of quality of life, quality of living, social functioning and overall functioning can be assessed. In essence, such measures required to achieve integration in the community could be introduced as a prelude for discharge. Obviously, outcome frameworks need to not be rigid, but required to be individualized and integrated in a clear package of a personalized treatment approach.

What, then, do such broadened outcomes include?

As psychiatric illnesses are complex and multifaceted, the approach to their treatment needs to be multimodal, generating a multitude of outcomes. Focusing on fewer outcomes deemed important in most of the available treatment approaches, six main outcomes evolved as the main targets, according to our ad priori criteria. Outcomes need to be demonstrated as valid and reliable, and important in dealing with aspects of the illness and its recovery. Selected outcomes ought to be based on conceptual thinking, and there exists adequate methodology for its reliable assessment. Employing such criteria, five major outcomes were chosen and include:

- quality of life
- subjective tolerability to medications
- satisfaction and preferences
- social functioning
- wellness psychiatry

Health-Related Quality of Life

Improved health-related quality of life is what patients, their families and physicians aspire to achieve as a result of medical and psychiatric clinical interventions. The *Quality of Life* construct is a complex psychosocial concept that had its origins in the economic prosperity and the enhanced standards of living that followed the end of the Second World War. Broadening the definition of health in 1947, the World Health Organization (WHO) included *mental health* in addition to *physical health*. Such a broadening of the concept of health brought in a number of psychological expectations, such as satisfaction and a sense of fulfillment and well-being, which were quickly picked up by social scientists and led to extensive population-based quality of life research, focused on social indicators. Though the concept of quality of life was vague and ill-defined, as described in 1976, by one of the leading social researchers, A. Campell, in a foreword of the major publication by the American Psychological Association, entitled "Subjective Measures of Well-being": "Quality of life...a vague and ethereal entity, something that many people talk about, but which nobody clearly knows what to do about it". As the concept got picked up by economists and politicians, the concept of quality of life became popularized and politicized. The well known book by the economist John Kenneth Galbraith, titled "The Affluent Society", led the way in 1964 for President Johnson to use it in his famous speech about the affluent society. As the concept achieved broad popularity, it became clear that the concept was too broad to allow for focused empirical research, since the feelings of well-being can encompass broad entities that could relate to diverse states and origins beyond good health. Narrowing the focus to "health-related quality of life", enhanced the ability to develop much more research effort focused on the development of conceptual models that underpin the concept and explore its determinants.

In psychiatry, the de-institutionalization of mental hospitals in the 1950s and early 1960s, which allowed for the precipitous discharges of chronic psychiatric residents of the asylums to communities that were not prepared to welcome them, added an impetus to the quick embracement of the concept of health-related quality of life in psychiatry. The poor and deteriorated living conditions of the unwelcomed chronic psychiatric patients in the community drew particular attention and focused research, and shed light on their tragic and sad plight. Such critical concerns were led by Leona Bacharach, a social scientist, and Anthony Lehman, a psychiatrist and health researcher. Both were credited for their pioneering work that brought issues of quality of life to mainstream psychiatric practices.

That was the point at which myself and my team entered the foray of quality of life in psychiatry, in the late 1970s. I became convinced that in order for the important concept of quality of life was to survive and impact psychiatric practices, it had to be approached as a scientific concept that required validation of the concept, and adapting it to some of the unique features of psychiatric disorders. How reliable are stable psychotic patients in describing their inner and subjective feelings, or formulating a reliable opinion about their level of satisfaction, which needed to be demonstrated. In short, the concept of quality of life became an important clinical and academic research focus at the centre of our broad academic priority interests: patient-centred research.

A part of providing evidence for validating the concept of quality of life in psychiatric patients and the development of conceptual models that led to the identification of the important factors that contribute to it, we were able to demonstrate how low quality of life was among psychiatric patients, particularly those with schizophrenia. To adhere to the original and pure definition of quality of life as a subjective construct, we separated the concept into two parts; the subjective component has been retained under the original title of "quality of life". The other component, named "quality of living", was to include all of the other issues, such as housing, financial, self-care, etc. The reason behind the separation was to delineate the origins of various factors that contribute to the concept, making it possible to design more practical corrective actions.

Following years of extensive research by Dr. Lakshmi Voruganti, myself and the team, and after contributing numerous academic and public presentations and publications, I am not only delighted with our contributions and its impact on the field of quality of life in psychiatry, but also have one serious regret. As the field became popular, as noted in the expansion of the numerous publications and the many conferences devoted to the topic, and including the development of specialized societies that promote quality of life issues in all medical fields, regrettably, a good majority of the research studies seemed to stop at the assessment stage. Much fewer studies proceeded beyond assessments and dealt with how to integrate the assessments into routine care plans. Such a clear deficit has led me to invite a number of experts in the field to address such an important gap, which was recently published in a book edited by me and my long-time colleague and contributor Lakshmi Voruganti, under the title "Beyond Assessment of Quality of Life in Schizophrenia".

On the positive and optimistic side, I can say that the concept of quality of life, particularly in major psychiatric disorders such as schizophrenia, continues to be a valid and important construct, reflecting the modern image of psychiatry. It is clear that enhancing quality of life and increasing the functional and social states of seriously ill psychiatric patients, can justify the costs involved and very likely can pay-off eventually, in terms of improved health outcomes and lower health expenditures. In the end, I believe that the concept of quality of life in medicine and psychiatry is no longer an ethereal or a vague concept, and it has already progressed and become an aspired goal of psychiatric treatment and other interventions.

Subjective Tolerability to Medications

Clearly patients would not continue to take their medications unless they feel right and comfortable on them. Medications, particularly in the case of schizophrenia and other psychotic conditions, have become the cornerstone of clinical management over the last few decades. That is why subjective tolerability to psychiatric medications matters. Unfortunately, a number of negative subjective responses to antipsychotic medications were noted shortly after the introduction of the first specific antipsychotic, chlorpromazine, in the early 1950s, as we detailed in another chapter. Patients reported feeling like zombies, dysphoric, unable to think straight and believing that the medications were making them sicker, and frequently requesting their discontinuation or warning they would discontinue the medication themselves. A number of subsequent clinical studies confirmed such worrisome observations, however the impact of the studies was lost, as these observations were invariably named in several publications as behavioural toxicity, akinetic depression or neuroleptic dysphoria. It was not until the late 1970s and early 1980s that the concept of subjective response to antipsychotics was clarified, after two separate and independent groups, one in the US led by Professors Philip May, Ted Van Putten and Steven Marder, and the other in Canada, represented by my research team that included Tom Hogan, Lakshmi Voruganti and Ron Heselgrave, published a series of clinical studies that defined the concept of subjective tolerability and outlined its serious sequences, in terms of medication adherence behaviour and its contribution to comorbid vulnerability to drug abuse behaviour.

In the process of validating the concept of subjective tolerability to psychiatric medications, we developed a reliable and validated tool for its measurement, the Drug Attitude Inventory, known as the DAI, and has served as the gold standard for the further development of other similar scales. Having a reliable measuring tool permitted us to propose a number of conceptual models, that informed of the possible determinants of the concept and their level of contribution. Though the neurotransmitter, dopamine, has always been suspected of being implicated in the emergence of dysphoric and negative subjective responses, it was not until the development of neuroimaging techniques that allowed us to explore the neurobiology of subjective tolerability. Our definitive study in late 1999, and published in early 2001, experimentally manipulating dopamine by depleting it in the brain and conducting a SPECT neuroimaging study, we were able to demonstrate for the first time a correlation between dysphoric responses and the dopamine binding ratio in the nigrostriatal area of the brain. As we continued the behavioural observation for forty-eight hours post-dopamine depletion, we witnessed the cascade of events that followed depletion, which was the equivalent of taking an antipsychotic medication, such as chlorpromazine. The first behavioural change shortly after the dopamine depletion was the subjective negative changes, followed by mood and motor changes, to be followed at last by cognitive state alterations. This is a typical sequence, as would be noted clinically after taking an antipsychotic medication. I do strongly believe that subjective tolerability to medications is an important outcome that needs to be fully recognized and evaluated. "The best medications are of little value unless they are tolerated and taken as prescribed".

Satisfaction and Preferences

Satisfaction and preferences are both important subjective constructs that are frequently used as indicators of the quality of health care provided. The construct of "satisfaction" is too broad to be meaningfully defined, unless it is anchored to a specific entity, such as medications, clinical care, community integration, etc. Preferences go a step beyond satisfaction, as it requires a degree of affective and cognitive intactness, in order to be able to make choices and decisions. As such, both constructs prove to be important tools in evaluating the overall quality of care, as "perceived" by the particular individual; the recipient of care. The ease of use of the concept of satisfaction has made it popular for inclusion in health surveys. The level of satisfaction can be elicited by a simple global question, such as, "How satisfied are you with the health care provided?", or using more structured items that can clarify aspects of the concept, that cannot be obtained by that one overall global single question.

In a recent visit to Sao Paolo, Brazil, at the invitation of professor Wagner Gattaz, Director of the Institute of Psychiatry, and the neuroscientist Professor Rodrigos Bressan at the University of Sao Paolo, I was hugely impressed by how the concept of satisfaction was used to provide an instantaneous evaluation of care received. On the way out from a clinic, patients are requested to express their evaluation of the visit by just pressing a button; yes or no. Certainly, an ingenious use of electronic technology.

The concept of "satisfaction" is rather complex and multifactorial, depending on the theoretical, ideological and psychological orientation. It is clear that "satisfaction" as a subjective, judgment overlaps with other subjective constructs, such as quality of life or subjective tolerability of medications. There seems to be a central core that cuts across such concepts, which is likely closer to the state of satisfaction. As frequently noted, an improvement in one subjective construct usually extends to improvement in other subjective states.

Obviously, a clearer understanding of the core of improvement in such subjective constructs, can augment the development of specific approaches towards the enhancement of such outcomes.

One of the notable conceptual models, among many others, has been what is known as the "gap model". According to this premise, satisfaction is defined as the gap between expectations and achievements, and the wider the gap, the lower the level of satisfaction. More recently, we introduced a clinically intuitive model, which we believe to be more applicable to clinical trials of new psychiatric medications. In this model, three factors are identified as major determinants of satisfaction with medications, which are clinical symptoms and their severity, subjective tolerability of medications, including their side effects and subjective quality of life. These factors are integrated in a circular model that emphasizes their interconnectedness, and their potential to impact each other. As interest in the concept of satisfaction in health care research has been rising in recent decades, several validated assessment tools were introduced, including the recent new scale *Medication Satisfaction Scale (MSQ)*. One of the most interesting observations using "satisfaction" as a primary outcome, measured by the MSQ in a clinical trial of a new antipsychotic medication, was that changes in the level of satisfaction was noted earlier than any other symptom changes, predicting a more favourable outcome. Such an interesting and unique observation is in line with the much earlier finding from our SPECT dopamine depletion study, that demonstrated that subjective changes were the earliest changes perceived by the patients after depleting dopamine (the equivalent of taking an antipsychotic pill), which was much earlier than other well established side effects, such as motor changes.

All in all, evaluation of satisfaction with care provided is certainly a major attribute of the level of quality of such services. I wonder how easy it is to include in the psychiatric interview a question about how satisfied patients are with the care received. To my surprise, in an informal survey we conducted among our own staff in one of the clinics, we discovered that such a question was not frequently directly asked, but was generally surmised from other collateral information. Using the Sao Paolo electronic model, providers can collect instant evaluations of the care provided. How easy and informative it could be!

Social Functioning

A decline in psychosocial functioning is well recognized as a central core of the schizophrenia disorder process, that can antedate the appearance of the earliest psychotic symptoms. Though there is not yet a full agreement on a clear definition about what is meant as social functioning, it is clear that any definition of social functioning has to include the capacity to function in different roles, such as vocational, recreational or interpersonal. Additionally, it is also expected to include the important notion of being able to derive some pleasure and satisfaction from social functioning, that proves to be helpful in achieving an integrative active role in society.

In schizophrenia, negative/deficit symptoms, as well as neurocognitive deficits, have been recognized as contributors to a decline in social functioning. Though the clusters of positive, negative and cognitive deficits are frequently associated together, evolving evidence from several studies, including one of ours, all point to the relative independence of such clusters from each other. The strength of such a psychopathological argument, at last has convinced the FDA to consider approval of medication-specific for the primary treatment of a single symptoms cluster, such as social functioning or neurocognitive deficits, as discussed in another chapter. It is clear that any significant improvement in social functioning cannot be expected with the use of medications alone, as it seems to require other additional interventions. In all our studies, we relied on the use of the Personal Social Scale (PSP), which is a well-validated scale in common use.

In summary, though the field of social functioning in the context of major psychiatric disorders still requires a good deal of informative research, it is an important component among the various outcomes that contribute to the process of recovery and integration in the community.

Wellness, Medicine and Psychiatry

I have to note from the outset, the concept of wellness in medicine has been around for a long time, but up until recently was obscured by its attractiveness as a commercial target. The wide and popular commercial use of the concept of *wellness*, from wellness strawberry jam to wellness jump suits, etc., have tended to blur the line between its use in science and its popular public use. Frequently and mistakenly, the concept of wellness has been referred to as an "alternative medicine". The reality is that concepts of wellness have for a long time been an extension of medicine, rather than an alternative, and that is what is evolving at the present time. For the concept to be useful in medicine and psychiatry, it has to be approached as a scientific construct that must be adapted to the specific conditions of individual disorders.

Wellness, as distinct from an improvement or feelings of satisfaction, is it being in a continuum that has no end, and thus becomes a process toward ever higher levels of wellness. Such a conceptualization tends to entrust a person with some responsibility in achieving and maintaining their own recovery, through the achievement of wellness.

The recent attention to such an encompassing concept in the management of psychiatric disorders has contributed to the development of several conceptual models, that have proven helpful in the design and use of new assessment tools, that certainly can enhance the grounding of the concept as a process for improvement and as a valued outcome to psychiatric interventions.

The recent publication edited by Professor Waguih William IsHak, "Handbook of Wellness Medicine", has provided a significant and inclusive reference book that surely will contribute to the refining of the concept of wellness in its application to various medical disorders, including psychiatric and addiction disorders. I am pleased to have contributed a chapter that dealt with psychiatric disorders, and look forward to expanding our research interests in the concept of wellness, as I do believe that it captures the sum of all accrued benefits following various interventions.

Improving Psychiatric Care: An Additional Cost, or an Investment for the Future?

One of the issues that occupied my thinking and my academic interests, besides the issues related to broadening and improving psychiatric outcomes, was the complex issue of "cost". In the management of a major psychiatric disorder, as in the case of schizophrenia, a positive outcome has to go beyond symptom improvement and the availability of better tolerated medications that have minimal or no side effects. It also needs to involve improvements in additional domains that include a better quality of life and quality of living, the ability for self-care and a return to a more productive role and fulfilling relationships with family and friends. Raising the quality of life for patients with schizophrenia or other major psychiatric disorders may seem at first to lead to higher costs, not only for expensive new psychiatric medications, but also for rehabilitation, living assistance, economic and housing support. It is clear that the higher quality of life achieved through treatment, the more likely the person suffering from schizophrenia, or other major psychiatric disorder, will become a productive member of society and not simply a source of large psychiatric expenditures and a recipient of life-long social and economic assistance, particularly that disorders like schizophrenia, usually have their onset early in life. In other words, the most cost-effective treatment is the one that brings about the greatest rehabilitation and the highest quality of life, even if it proves more expensive in the short-term. The alternative would be frequent psychotic relapses that require frequent hospitalizations, which are the most expensive component of psychiatric care. And that is the crux of the cost issue.

Conscious about the escalating cost of psychiatric care, and at the same time with the realization that psychiatric care budgets were historically very low, I became convinced that cost-containment, such as cost-effective studies, needed to become an important outcome in its own right. That statement quickly proved to be easily said and more complex to be done, when it comes to psychiatric disorders. The direct costs, such as hospitalizations and the follow-up care, proved to be easier to count, compared to the multitudes of indirect care, including lost productivity and burden of care costs to family and carers, both requiring complex methodologies, which were mostly lacking.

That was enough of a challenge for our team to get involved in cost-benefit methodologies, focusing on cost-utility analysis. Considering the high cost of the new antipsychotics and antidepressants compared to the historically cheap Chlorpromazine and similar old medications, we didn't have a reliable handle on the cost of new antipsychotics related to comparative benefits, and there was the concern that patients may miss the opportunity of receiving more benefit from the new medications. So we decided to proceed with cost-utility analysis, among the many other methodologies, as it could give a clear comparative figure value among the new antipsychotics. Our objectives were many-fold, including the two main questions of whether it was at all feasible to conduct utility analysis among stable patients with schizophrenia, and whether the patients could judge various health states and assign values to them in a reliable and valid way, both of which were the central elements at the core of utility analysis.

Surprisingly, we were able to complete the study, enrolling over 120 patients. In spite of its complexities, it seemed the patients enjoyed it, as the feedback they gave described it as an enjoyable electronic game. Though our results confirmed the feasibility of cost-utility analysis in schizophrenia, we harboured some reservations about whether such a complex methodology would become popular or accepted by clinicians. The methodology proved difficult to follow and the results were often expressed in language that impeded communication and understanding. Exploring the results of the comparisons in figures, instead of providing a profile of the effects of the interventions under study, proved to have significant limitations. In general, our eventual recommendation for the use of such a complex methodology was to get clinicians working closely with health economists, to understand each other's language and perspectives. I felt that was the only way to learn how to translate utility analysis results into meaningful information for clinical decision making. Nevertheless, I strongly believe that the utility approach is attractive and valid, and should be further explored.

Such a conclusion was communicated to a small group of expert clinicians and prominent health economists in a closed round table symposium held in Chicago, on April 8, 1998, and co-chaired by Professor Herbert Meltzer and Professor Willard G. Manning, Jr. In the extensive discussions that followed my presentation, and at the end of the day, there seemed to be a sound agreement on the value of using utility measures in schizophrenia, but that it required further studies to make it user friendly and more applicable. Almost twenty years later, I was somewhat astounded as I reviewed the 1999 issue of The Journal of Clinical Psychiatry, in which the presentations and discussions of the closed symposium were published including my article titled "Pharmacoeconomic Factors Related to the Treatment of Schizophrenia". If I could magically change the date of that issue to 2020, the article would be current and up-to-date regarding the continued unresolved challenges in cost-benefit assessments and the higher cost of the new medications. It seems that some concerns tend to linger for a long time without adequate resolution, simply by ignoring them and moving on to other issues, resulting in a significant waste of time, resources and missed opportunity

PART IX

Current Psychiatric Practices

How Psychiatry is Failing Many: The Patients, Their Doctors, Their Families and Society at Large

Modern psychiatry truly had its beginning in the late 1940s and the early 1950s. It was ushered in by the transformational discovery of the first specific antipsychotic medication Chlorpromazine, on the clearly waning background of the psychoanalytic doctrine that captured psychiatric thinking and practice for several decades. Such a major discovery had allowed for the final demise of the asylum concept with the following shift of psychiatric care from the asylums to communities, which were not adequately equipped to welcome and support the precipitously discharged chronic asylum patients. For science it was a triumphant event of a major discovery, but in practice it proved to be a major logistical failure that seemed to cripple the development of an appropriate psychiatric service for a long time to afterward. Mapping progress over the past seven decades, since the major peak of scientific progress in the early 1950s, the course of progress did not proceed in a straight line, as was expected. It was more like distinct short peaks of progress and optimism, separated by rather long and basically stagnant valleys of little or no significant progress.

By the early 1970s, biological psychiatry seemed to establish some of its early roots, slowly displacing the longstanding psychoanalytic influences, both in academia and in practice. At the same time, what is now known as the "anti-psychiatry movement" made a strong appearance, led by its two major rebels, R.D. Laing and Thomas Szasz. The publication of Thomas Szasz's book "The Myth of Mental

Illness" was widely received, but also met with broad and harsh criticism. Meanwhile, communities continued to struggle with so many discontented psychiatric patients protesting their inadequate and mostly ineffective treatments, as well as their poor living conditions. Families were increasingly burdened by frequently assuming the patient care. Communities and society at large were unable to adequately fund a disorganized and poorly coordinated psychiatric health care system. In response, the policy- and decision-making authorities established a long series of commissions, panels, task forces, etc., for the purpose of reforming the failing mental health system. In the past forty years, I was able to count more than thirty such high level commissions and task forces that introduced a wide range of recommendations, but only a few were implemented and then given enough time to judge their value.

In the last twenty years alone, several important commissions were introduced and given resounding and lofty titles. The long list includes such commissions as: Making It Happen (1999), Mental Health – the Next Steps (2000), Making It Happen (2001), Mental Health Implementation Task Force (2002/2003), Out of the Shadows at Last (2006), Moving in the Right Direction (2009), Every Door is the Right Door (2009), Towards Recovery and Wellness (2009), Open Minds (2011), Changing Directions (2012), Open Mind, Healthy Mind (2014), Better Mental Health Means Better Health (2015), Taking Stock – A report of the quality of Mental Health Services (2015), and so on. With the rapid succession and the almost overlapping of many of them, on the surface they look commendable for their keen objectives, but in reality the situation pointed to a fundamental error: In implementing such a plethora of reports and not giving them enough time to be effective, along with the frequent changes in course and directions, has certainly left a deep impression of how discontinuous the course of reforms has been. It is well known to those familiar with the inner workings of such high level commissions and task forces, their reports are mostly and generally based on broad aggregates of statistics and information that is frequently hard to distill down to local or individual levels. I do believe that, in spite of the plethora of such significant reports, sadly, not much has seriously changed in either the organization or quality of psychiatric care.

Current psychiatric practices continue to fail many: the patients, their doctors, their families and society at large. Meanwhile, I also strongly believe that reforms starting from the bottom, not only from the top, can deliver more serious and practical proposals for reforms.

Here, I will highlight the many concerns at the core of the real day-to-day psychiatric care process, as seen from the perspective of the principal recipient of care, the patient.

The Patient

In recent decades "patient-centred care" has evolved as the optimal approach for the provision of health care. The innovative and pioneering efforts in 1987, of the development in the US of The Picker/Commonwealth Patient-Centred Care Program has popularized the concept, backed by their extensive research data confirming its value in promoting much more appropriate health care. The excellent book by Margaret Gertis and her colleagues published in 1993, *Through the Patients Eyes*, based on research data generated by the Picker-Commonwealth program, not only outlined the details of what is meant by patient-centred care, but also identified the individual dimensions of the concept itself. Defining its conceptual framework, it included seven important dimensions that are considered the major contributing components: respect for patients' values, preferences and expressed needs, coordination and integration of care, information communication, education, physical comfort, emotional support and alleviation of fear and anxiety, involvement of family and friends and, lastly, the issue of transition and continuity. This conceptual model with its seven dimensions has served as the standard for judging the appropriateness of health care, and I use them to evaluate the current quality and organization of psychiatric care. Several other health scientists, including some major contributions from our psychiatric research team, have taken the concept of patient-centred care in its application to psychiatric care, defined the concept and developed appropriate methodologies for its assessment.

Central to the concept of patient-centred care, patients and their families have to be listened to and have their complaints and concerns to be seriously considered. Applying such a requirement to the current practice of psychiatry, patients are struggling with a multitude of concerns, many of which are serious enough to undermine the process of care. High on the list of complaints is the clear statement of patients' dissatisfaction with psychiatric treatments, whether due to medications, psychotherapy, rehabilitation programs or the lack of them.

• Medications

Medications, old or new, are at best partly effective or not effective at all. Taking the case of antipsychotic medications, for example, they can be helpful mostly for a limited range of symptoms known as the "positive symptoms", such as agitation, hallucinatory or paranoid experiences, but have little or no impact on other important groups of symptoms referred to as the "negative" or "deficit" symptoms, as well as a range of cognitive deficits. Feeling apathetic, lacking motivation, unable to feel or function appropriately on medications constitutes a major limitation and a challenge. The same can be said about various antidepressant medications, old and new. At best they are marginally better than placebos and carry a significant range of serious side effects liability, such as excessive weight gain or impaired sexual functioning. Antipsychotics can also have similar serious side effects, some of which are in the category of inconvenience, such as dry mouth, constipation, sedation, but other serious neurological side effects, such as body rigidity, tremors or tardive dyskinesia, which can be permanent and disfiguring. Worse, the new generation of antipsychotic has brought a new range of serious side effects that include obesity, metabolic and hormonal alterations, such as diabetes, cardiovascular and endocrine problems that can pose serious health risks. Since the medications have to be taken for a long time, almost life-long, the prolonged exposure to such risks can complicate management and undermine general health. Attempts to minimize long term exposure to medications by exploring the feasibility of a medication holiday or intermittent course has failed, following inconclusive research results. I believe this issue needs to be revisited and more rigorous study designs need to be explored. I do believe that such an exploration has been prematurely abandoned, but could benefit from the new thinking of the psychopathology as associated, but rather, independent groups of symptoms. Not withstanding all these side effects and concerns, the new psychiatric medications are more expensive and the high cost certainly represents a barrier for access to new treatment approaches.

For decades, new medication development has mostly focused on symptoms improvement as the primary outcome in response to the medications. Though improvement in symptoms is critical, by themselves it is not enough to achieve other important outcomes such as improvement in the functional state, including social functioning and other related issues important for the needs of the person behind the illness. Some of these needs require involvement in rehabilitative programs, in addition to medications and psychotherapy. Major psychiatric disorders such as schizophrenia or bipolar disorder, as multidimensional disorders, accordingly, require multimodal treatment approaches. The lack of availability and low funding for psychiatric rehabilitation programs not only complicates the process of recovery, but certainly adds to the state of disability that frequently becomes permanent. Regrettably, rehabilitation budgets are generally the first to be hit in situations of budget adjustments, which is short-sighted and more costly in the long run. A good example of how rehabilitation efforts can be more economic reminds me of one of the best examples that supports such a contention. Several years back, I attended to a patient in his mid-forty years who suffered from schizophrenia at an early age, when he was a university student. Fortunately, he was diagnosed early and successfully engaged in treatment that included serious psychiatric rehabilitation efforts. His rehabilitation program included a technique called "dissimulation", teaching the patient on how to suppress some symptoms, such as responding to hearing voices. At the time I saw him in consultation for a medication adjustment, he had already been functioning as a librarian in a large city library for three years. His ability to suppress his auditory hallucinations from nine-to-five, during his working hours, had helped him to function and stave off his disability. I have to say I have not seen many such cases in recent years, which I attribute in large part to a lack of accessibility to serious and effective rehabilitation programs.

• Medical Psychotherapy

Equally disturbing has been the issue of psychotherapy, the important second arm in the armamentarium of psychiatric treatments.

Psychotherapy is in a state of chaos with over four-hundred types or approaches available, most of which are not conceptually based and have never been validated. More often, many of them have been influenced by trends or fads. Psychotherapy tends to be lengthy and frequently is open-ended and, as such, is costly and only available for the few. As frequently criticized, psychotherapy is provided in uneven levels of expertise and competence, which at times raises the important question of whether anyone can be a psychotherapist? The answer is mostly "yes", even with minimal qualifications or inadequate training. That raises the other question: who ensures competent practices? Sadly as one patient commented on her psychotherapy experience as being unsatisfactory: "My hairdresser gave me more sensible advice for much less cost". There was time when departments of psychiatry in general hospitals used to include in their staffing a few positions for psychologists, who usually provided psychological services, including the supervision of psychotherapy. Such positions, unfortunately, do not exist anymore in most of the departments of psychiatry, mainly due to a lack of funding, but also not excluding some territorial conflicts.

Among psychiatrists, not many who are experts and specialized in a psychotherapy. In reality most of the psychotherapy provided in a general psychiatric practice is nothing more than low level counselling that could be provided by less qualified, but trained professionals. For seekers of psychotherapy, the frequent pressing and challenging question is how to choose a psychotherapist. The question then becomes; psychotherapy for whom, by whom, what type, how long and at what cost?

The recent evolvement of time-limited, behaviourally-based and validated psychotherapeutic approaches have been a welcome addition. It requires special expert training and funding. A few years ago, a senior administration colleague in our hospital consulted me about his high anxiety and fears of flying, to the point that at the age of forty-five he had never set foot in an airplane, which was very limiting to him professionally. After a referral to an expert cognitive therapist and a few sessions, he is comfortably enjoying what he had missed for years. Fortunately, the process was facilitated by him being covered with extra private insurance that allowed him to access the services quickly, rather than being stuck on a waiting list for publicly-funded services. That raises the question of why a proven, evidence based and economic psychotherapeutic approach is not adequately publicly funded, whereas many other less validated, lengthy and costly approaches are well funded and recognized. In fact, the value of what is provided as psychotherapy in general psychiatric practices tends to be questionable. More and more research evidence has demonstrated that a good deal of "talk therapy" is of less value, unless it is accompanied by cognitive enhancing approaches. We also reported similar findings in our research regarding the role of medication educational sessions in improving medication compliance behaviour. Our conclusion, similarly, was that the value of such educational sessions was low, unless it was accompanied by cognitive remedial approaches.

To complicate matters is the reimbursement for medical psychotherapy, including at times the questionable three to four year courses limited only to psychiatrists, not many of whom are truly well trained as expert psychotherapists. And those psychiatrists who are truly experts are frequently unavailable or burdened already by high demand. The reality is that there exists other professionals with equally high levels of expertise in psychotherapy, but they are not reimbursed by national health schemes. Interesting enough, even among medical professionals, such as medical general practitioners and family physicians who received training and are well qualified as psychotherapists, are compensated at a lower rate. In recent years several general practitioners have been practicing exclusively as psychotherapists and belong to the recently developed and successful "General Practitioners Psychotherapy Association", that takes care of qualifications and other professional requirements. Certainly, they can fill the gap left in psychiatric practices and make psychotherapy more available, but then their financial compensation needs to be revisited. It is clear that such issues of equity and equality in the field of psychotherapy are raising tensions and resentment among professionals, but worse, the urgent need for access to available competent and expert psychotherapy is not met.

In view of the importance of the role of psychotherapy in psychiatric treatment and the several inherent problems in its practice, particularly the issues of access and competency, I wonder whether it is time to consider psychotherapy as an independent field that can stand on its own and requires being regulated by a type of academy or professional board? Such a development would ensure qualifications, expertise and equitable remuneration among certified members of the board or academy, and would also take care of the important issues of maintenance of competence and promotion of a strong academic base.

Indeed, several European academic departments of psychiatry have already the title of "Department of Psychiatry and Psychotherapy". Obviously, such a designation of psychotherapy as an associated, but independent field, has implications for how academic departments are organized, as well as its impact on psychiatrists' incomes. At present, the most recent income averages among medical specialists put psychiatry at or close to the bottom. I believe psychiatry deserves to be better positioned, otherwise it would be difficult to attract some of the strong medical students as applicants for psychiatry as a career option.

• **Psychiatric Resources and Manpower Distribution**

Disparities in the distribution of resources and manpower are clearly noted, not only between urban and rural regions, but within a region between hospital-based funding and the community. In recent years there have been significant enhancements of hospital-based psychiatric services represented by the increase in bed capacity, which is the most expensive component of the psychiatric care spectrum. Though changes in bed capacity have needed to adjust for population changes in several regions, it has been interesting to note that once more beds were added, they were in no time over-occupied and the need for more beds became pressing.

It is becoming obvious that the continuous pressure for more beds is a bottomless issue and there will never be enough. A better explanation for such an expensive phenomenon is that adding more and more beds is not the real answer. I would argue that the real answer can only be found in developing more appropriate alternatives to hospitalizations in the community or even in the hospital itself.

There was a time not long ago when there was more enthusiasm and interest in developing programs for partial hospitalizations. Several models of "day hospitals", as distinct from daycare programs, were introduced, with a high level of success. Unfortunately, over the years the concept of partial hospitalizations slowly declined as a result of misuse and mismanagement.

Instead of correcting and refining the gaps and learning from mistakes, the model of partial hospitalizations was abandoned. It resulted in the creation of a much bigger bed capacity in general hospitals, at the expense of other mandated clinical responsibilities, such as the provision of consultative psychiatric services to the medical and surgical programs and embedding psychiatry in a few of their teams. Additionally, outpatient hospital clinics have become crowded, requiring unacceptably long waiting times, up to six months or longer. There is no more room nor funds to develop new programs, or to even update the old clinics. Emergency psychiatric clinics are generally overwhelmed by demands of crisis and urgent services. Such an unhelpful and worrisome picture of general hospital psychiatry clearly demonstrates that the policy of adding more beds is not working nor doing the intended job.

The development of departments of psychiatry in general hospitals continues to be an important model of care and certainly needs to be preserved, but not in its current practice. I believe the concept needs to be revisited, in order to save it. Many of its functions need to be shifted to the community. Models of integrated care in the community need to be explored, as for example, in line with the previously mentioned Multiservice York Community Centre, in Toronto. Departments of psychiatry in general hospitals have to be centres for complex and specialized innovative care. They need to be the academic back-up and a leader of excellence. For rural and remote regions, the recent development of regional academic centres and universities has improved access to professional and stable services available on location. Technological advances, such as telemedicine has helped to close the gap and allowed for remote access to specialized psychiatric consultations. For regions close to urban centres, general hospital academic centres need to take the responsibility of formally supporting them in the provision of specialized care.

• Stigma and its Negative Impacts

The stigma of mental illness has existed for as long as mental illness has existed. Though I recognize that there has been some improvement in stigmatizing-behaviour in recent years, following several successful anti-stigma campaigns, stigma has not gone away. In a recent survey we conducted among health professionals, we were dismayed by the amount of stigmatizing words and attitudes that were recorded. It is clear that anti-stigma approaches are a long term goal that not only needs periodic booster follow-up campaigns, but also requires frequent adjustments and ensure balance. As one of our long-term psychiatric patients expressed his feelings, "I prefer to be treated like everyone else, as I am uncomfortable to be singled out by the extra attention I am getting!". Whether getting extra attention or no attention at all, the majority of the seriously afflicted psychiatric patients live in an utter state of loneliness. In another survey among patients attending one of our psychiatric clinics, we asked them to rank the top ten concerns they were struggling with. Surprisingly, loneliness was ranked as the top concern. One patient commented, "I would very much feel better if I had a friend I could go with for a coffee". We, as physicians, are quick to issue a prescription for medications, but rarely, if ever, do we fill a prescription for loneliness, such as a referral for recreational activity or socializing.

Equally concerning, is the ability to gain access to crisis intervention in the community, leaving presenting to the emergency department at a nearby hospital as the only quick option. As urgent psychiatric assessments are frequently deemed to be not as urgent as some of the medical or life-threatening medical interventions, a psychiatric assessment can take most of a day, unless the situation involves violent behaviour. Such an unacceptable situation has raised an important issue about whether the need for the separation of emergency psychiatric assessments, to be conducted in a completely separate location, can improve access and quality. Apart from the cost, such a proposal would take us back to when psychiatry was segregated from the rest of medicine. It also denies or delays the provision of medical care to psychiatric patients in crisis, who frequently are also in need of medical attention. The most appropriate solution is to deploy crisis intervention teams in a separate area of the emergency departments, where a few short-stay beds can be located. Such a model can justify its cost by improving the care and lowering inpatient admissions, easing the pressure on crowded hospital inpatient beds.

The Doctor

The role of the psychiatrist is continuously being challenged and eroded from the top by other qualified professionals' increasing pressure for an expanded share of services, particularly in the field of psychotherapy. On the other hand, serious unmet clinical and scientific needs challenge the role of the psychiatrist at the base.

- **The Definition of Mental Health and the Role of the Psychiatrist**

The definition of mental health and the role of the psychiatrist has been clearly detailed in the World Health Organization (WHO) Expert Committee on Mental Health report, in 1950. As the terms "mental health" and "psychiatric disorders" have been synonymously used, the 1950 WHO clarification adopted a distinction by separating the terms and assigning psychiatry as a major part of mental health. Further more, the role of the psychiatrist was clearly defined as a "medical specialist who deals with the study, diagnosis, treatment and prevention of psychiatric disorders". Certainly, such a broad definition requires a broad range of skills that need to be based on a progressive and active research enterprise, as well as on equally progressive and appropriate training programs.

• The Lack of Strong Science

The lack of strong science that can back psychiatric practices tends to leave psychiatrists feeling vulnerable and not well-grounded in a solid scientific base. In spite of years of extensive research, the absence of etiological breakthroughs in the psycho-biology of major psychiatric disorders, such as schizophrenia or major depression and bipolar disorders, point to several fundamental gaps and whether they're due to a lack of theory or a misdirected search, or likely both. It is clear that for a major scientific breakthrough to happen, it has to be based on solid foundational basic science research that is grounded in an equally solid theoretical and conceptual framework, aided by the availability of the right technological tools.

It has been over a century since the diagnosis of schizophrenia was introduced, but it continues to be an etiological mystery. Did the eminent neuropathologist Emil Kraepelin, followed by the equally eminent Eugene Bleuler, get it wrong nosologically? Has the well-recognized problem in modern classificatory schemes, such as the DSM system, complicated the search by introducing artificial and non-valid groupings of symptoms that may have misdirected the search? Would a dimensional approach have a better chance of success, particularly since psychotic symptoms cut across several psychiatric conditions besides schizophrenia, such as dementia, delirium or drug-induced? I do recognize the complexity of designing a perfect or more appropriate classification system, particularly as a diagnosis is the starting point of any etiological research study. I do believe that there is a value in attempting to deconstruct major psychiatric disorders, such as schizophrenia. Going backward, in order to move forward.

That reminds me of a pleasant, but critical, encounter I had with the late Sir Martin Roth in October 1995, during a brief afternoon walk in Montreaux, on Lake Geneva, in between sessions of a conference regarding "Recent Advances in Psychiatric Treatments", a program in which both of us participated. When discussing the enormous challenges in developing an appropriate classification scheme, Sir Martin compared it to "how much more food companies profit from how much prepared mustard is left on the plate". His aphorism, he explained, cuts across nosological and phenomenological grounds. Eliminating too much detail and focusing only on the essentials, for a distinct and narrow diagnostic definition, can be a major challenge that requires leaving out many other details. How true his statement proved to be?

Another serious challenge in making good research progress has been the methodological issues, in terms of availability of the appropriate medical technological tools. There is an urgent need to invest adequately in the ongoing upgrade and development of newer technological tools. Equally important, is to rethink the optimum composition of research teams, to match current knowledge and new thinking. In addition to basic neuroscientists, psychiatrists and neurologists, modern neuroscience research teams need to include physicists, mathematicians, computer and communication scientists, medical philosophers and ethicists. The research challenges are enormous and raise the question of whether we are equipped to tackle it. There is a lot that we need urgently to know in basic neurosciences that can serve as the scientific foundation for building more successful clinical science research.

Presently, we are just at the beginning of a long and challenging scientific journey. This reminds me of an interesting science debate that took place in the mid-1990s, initiated by the publication of a book entitled "The End of Science", by the well-known science writer John Horgan. The book captured a good deal of attention in no time, but also attracted even more critical reviews and heated debate. One of the several "counter" books published, as a rebuttal, was a book by the well-known past editor of "Nature", the late Sir John Maddox, titled "What Remains to be Discovered". With the heated debates in various science circles, I felt they could be relevant to psychiatry, in shedding a focused light on psychiatric research and exposing the major gaps and limitations. My aim was to stimulate an international debate among scientists and clinicians, on how to move forward the psychiatric research enterprise to deal with the many pressing problems in psychiatric science and practice, but also to dispel any negative misinterpretation of John Horgan's book. I was fortunate to be able to invite and introduce Sir Maddox to the audience of scientists and clinicians attending the Schizophrenia Workshop in Davos, Switzerland, in February 2000. His presentation was followed by an extensive debate that highlighted the significant gaps in research strategies in psychiatry. It is clear that we need new strategies with longer time lines and based on new thinking. The extensively developed digital electronics field as also the quickly rising approaches in Artificial Intelligence (AI) advances compel us to think differently.

• Deficits in Curricula of Psychiatric Training

The other major and important issue for psychiatrists has been the gaps and deficits in the curricula of psychiatric training, which continue to a large extent to be modelled and padded by the mostly outdated psychoanalytic concepts. The abandonment of compulsory training in neurology in several countries, including in Canada, has produced generations of psychiatrists who are unable to follow progress in neurosciences. While psychiatry was historically leading with its psychodynamic approaches, neurology has in recent decades already claimed the development of "behavioural neurology", which is not much different than our "neuropsychiatry", and which is at present garnering little psychiatric research interest and training. In recent years more and more expert voices, from both neuropsychiatry and behavioural neurology, have been advocating for both fields to join efforts with a few experts, even calling for an outright merger. The lack of adequate training in clinical neurosciences has produced psychiatrists who are frequently unable to explain to patients and their families how psychiatric disorders are connected to brain functions. The most frequently used concept in psychiatry, and even as a term, "stress" is rather difficult for many psychiatrists to explain or conceptually and clearly define to patients.

In spite of the extensive information available about the rational use of the relatively small number of available psychiatric medications, survey after survey, including ours in 1991, revealed several below par psychopharmacological practices. Under-medicating, for fear of side effects, or overdosing due to impatience in giving medications adequate time, as well as polypharmacy were among the concerns revealed. Using multiple medications is not, by itself, good or bad, but its reason and purpose has to be clear. Lack of the ability to critically read and translate research publications was another frequent gap finding.

- **Who oversee the Science and Practice of Psychiatry?**

The absence in many countries, including Canada, of specialized academic and professional bodies that specifically deal with psychiatry and its needs, similar to the Royal College of Psychiatrists, in the UK, is a major gap. In Canada, such functions are assumed by The Royal College of Physicians and Surgeons of Canada (RCPSC), and the Canadian Psychiatric Association (CPA), which in reality is more like a labour union and its membership is indeed less than half of practicing psychiatrists in Canada. It is clear that psychiatry interests are squeezed out of The Royal College of Physicians and Surgeons of

Canada by the big players; surgery, medicine and their subspecialties. To be fair to the CPA, some improvement has recently been noted in their continuing education programs, but not enough to shake the image and functioning of an old, discontinuous organizational structure that is not equipped to provide a high level of academic expertise. For psychiatry to move forward and meet the so-many challenges the discipline is facing, a specialized and independent body, like a Canadian College of Psychiatry, is urgently needed.

Clinically, the average psychiatrist is burdened by work load and demands of services, spending a good deal of time attending to extensive follow-ups, which could be managed by other trained, but less qualified, professionals. Indeed, the rationale for how long a follow-up is required, which at times can be life-long, is not clear in the way it is practiced. It is an assumed practice, and has never been subjected to a clear evaluation.

• Lack of Interest in Consultation Psychiatry

Another practice issue has been the frequent reluctance of many psychiatrists to provide psychiatric consultations. By definition, a psychiatric consultation is conducted within a limited time and leads to the formulation of a diagnostic opinion and clear recommendations for management. Patients usually give us a lot of information, and the challenge for the psychiatrist is how quickly they are able to separate what is important from the less important or irrelevant. In other words, it's the clinical acumen of separating the wheat from the chaff. It is a clinical skill that can be acquired or improved by training, and that is why I tend to believe that some of the reluctance to engage in an appropriate consultative practice is likely related to the lack of adequate training. I am also frequently amazed by how poor consultation reports can be, in terms of a lack of clarity and unusual length, which can be up to several pages. A consultation report is not a copy of the lengthy psychiatric history. A busy practitioner most likely has time only to focus on the last paragraph, which represents the diagnostic formulation and recommendations. The long waiting time to see a psychiatrist for a consultation is not acceptable. A patient who is able to wait for over six months for a psychiatric consultation, in reality does not need to see a psychiatrist.

Major radical shifts in the patterns of psychiatric practices have been frequently noted, for no good reason or with evidence to justify it. One notable recent example is in the child and adolescent psychiatric fields. Years ago, we used to beg child and adolescent psychiatrists to use low doses of medication, in certain clinical situations. At present, we are still begging them, but now it's to rationalize their excessive use of medications.

- **Prevention in Psychiatry is Missing in Action**

Prevention in psychiatry, unfortunately, continues to be missing in action. Though, etiologically, we continue to be unclear about origins of major psychiatric disorders, we already have a good idea regarding several predisposing factors that can impact development, as well as the course of such disorders. Obviously, the best time to look and deal with such a predisposition has to be in the early years, otherwise, we miss the opportunity. A few years ago, in the course of an academic visit to the Department of Psychiatry at Fudan University in Shanghai, China, a city of over twenty million, I was pleasantly surprised by their well-developed school screening program, which starts as early as grade three and continues through all school years until graduation. Indeed, I was given the unusual opportunity to meet with a school team in one of the districts, and learn first hand how thorough their screening and follow up was. A costly model, but in the long run it justifies its costs. Why is such a great idea missing in most of the western countries? In all of my years I only recall one such project, conducted by Professor Harvey Golombek at University of Toronto, which as a research study followed a cohort of students from their early school years to graduation. The project yielded valuable data and several useful interventions, but, unfortunately, was terminated due to lack of funding.

I do believe that the role of the psychiatrist needs to be revisited and redefined, in terms of whether the role of the psychiatrist in the 21st century and beyond is just for a talking and empathic healer or a medical specialist in brain and behaviour? Most likely for most general psychiatrists, a good mix of both. Equally important is to remap the boundaries of psychiatry and not to let it become the treatment of all societal ills.

In essence, then, it is clear that the lack of a strong backing from science and the pressures of increasing demands, in the face of inadequate training and the limited resources in a fragmented service model, have failed many psychiatrists, leading to a noticeable state of dissatisfaction and quick burnout.

The Family

Being shamed and at times blamed for their children's psychiatric disorders, families feel significantly burdened by assuming the responsibility of care. Historically, the precipitous emptying of the mental asylums has de-facto shifted a major part of the burden of care to families and communities, without adequate support provided. As will be explored later in the detailed review of the concept of "burden of care", such a concept has been demonstrated to frequently extol a high price and has a negative impact emotionally, physically and medically, particularly in a highly fragmented psychiatric care system. Though patients' and caregivers' perspectives on care are often overlapping, there can be serious differences that require reconciliation to achieve some balance, as will be outlined later. Issues like violence, low self-care, lack of insight and motivation are among the frequent issues that require the involvement of the family in the process of care. Unfortunately, the role of the family is frequently missing as a result of the disintegration of the family unit or through the individual's estrangement. The economic impacts of family burden of care are extensive, but frequently are poorly captured or are computed incorrectly, such as being the "intangibles" in the cost of schizophrenia, as will be critically detailed in the following "review".

- **Family Burden of Care in Schizophrenia:**
  A Huge Emotional and Physical Cost, But
  Still Costed Among the "Intangibles"

The concept of "Burden of Care" is a broad and a complex construct that is defined by its impact and consequences. In addition to physical, psychological and economic consequences, it involves a range of subtle, distressing notions such as shame, embarrassment, guilt and self-blame. Though it has gained wide attention over recent decades, it still lacks clear costing among the direct and indirect costs of schizophrenia being costed among the "intangibles"!

As we detailed in our extensive review on the concept of burden of care in 2008, the origins of the concept appeared in the early years of the 20th century. In 1927, the writings of the influential psychiatrist Harry Stack Sullivan postulated, without clear evidence, that the origins of behaviour in schizophrenia are likely related to abnormal family interactions. For the next three decades, several theories evolved, after assigning a negative role to the mother, which is exemplified by the later debunked concepts of the schizophrenogenic mother, marital skew and schism or psychomutuality. Those and many other such theories were eventually abandoned, but not before shaming and distressing several generations of mothers and caregivers. On the other hand, the development of the concept of "expressed emotions" by G.W. Brown in the UK, shifted attention to the impact of the family and family environment. However, the most dramatic development that brought forward the concept of "burden of care" took place in the 1950s, following the introduction of Chlorpromazine and the end of traditional institutional care. The precipitous discharge of long-term psychiatric patients to a community that was ill-prepared to receive them, resulted in many families having no choice but to assume the role of caregiver. Even if the patient did not live with the family, intense involvement has been frequently required, in terms of emotional and financial support or dealing with crisis and safety. The shift to community-based psychiatric services has almost formalized the role of family and caregivers. The family and caregivers' role has thus been integrated in the treatment plans and policy-making decisions. The emergence of the "recovery movement", started in the 1970s, added impetus to the development of the family therapy approaches, with special focus on the role of family and the burden of care.

The role of family in the care of mentally ill patients and the ensuing burden of care has been increasingly acknowledged in a number of formal health policy documents, such as the President's New US Freedom Commission on Mental Health in 2003, or in the European Community policies in 2000. Nevertheless, families and caregivers continue to struggle, without adequate support or resources. Such a worrisome and disconcerting state was behind our major undertaking to join together in researching the concept of "burden of care" as an important part of our arching research program about quality of care, and broadening outcomes of psychiatric treatments. Our clear decision was based on a clear conviction that "burden of care" is an integral component of the overall care.

Our studies had the objectives of understanding, explaining and predicting healthcare attitudes and behaviours of the persons affected with schizophrenia, their families and caregivers. The landmark study was community-based longitudinal with follow-up over four years, that involved over eight hundred consenting patients with schizophrenia and over 1300 consenting caregivers. The methodology employed a number of self-administered questionnaires that included Care Giving Burden Scale, the Psychological General Well-Being Index, the SF-12 Health Survey and our Drug Attitude Inventory (DAI). As we expected, the majority of caregivers were mothers, as is usually the case. They were diverse, with multi-ethnic backgrounds and 80% of them reported to be very involved in the provision of care of their children afflicted with schizophrenia.

The burden of care-giving was high, giving on average a score of 2.7 out of 5 as the highest score. A detailed account of the impact of care-giving was informative in illustrating the burden and serious impacts of caring for a person with schizophrenia, in terms of decline in family social outings, increase in family fights and disagreements, cancellation of vacation plans and various economic difficulties. Family impact was equally concerning in that they included depression and anxiety in other family members, loss of self-esteem and embarrassment of other family members, decline in the work or school performance of other family members, as well as an increase in alcohol consumption. It was interesting that events of separation from a spouse were reported as low as only 1%. Most likely, the enormity of the crisis and the many other challenges seemed to have pulled parents together, in spite of the many discords and fights. Negative impact on physical and emotional health was reflected by the increased visits to doctors and emergency clinics or hospitalizations. Impaired personal, social and vocational role performance, as well as low quality of life and satisfaction were rather common.

To complicate matters, parents and caregivers frequently experienced conflicting perspectives. Asking caregivers to list and rank critical issues that they felt to be contributing to the perception of burden and stress, noncompliance and treatment adherence was ranked as the most frustrating, followed by lack of motivation and self-care, comorbid substance abuse, inadequate social and economic support and access to crisis psychiatric care or hospitalization when required. On the other hand, persons with schizophrenia perceived different issues as their significant problems. The most problematic for patients was identified as the need for access to more effective and better tolerated medications, followed by the expectation for patients to take medications indefinitely, almost life-long, quality of life and better functioning, stigma and opportunity for employment and social support and housing. It became clear from such diverse perspectives that there is an urgent need to have a balance and reconciliation of different expectations, in order to improve coping and facilitate recovery.

I have been pleasantly surprised by the response to our publication in the Journal of Pharmacoeconomics in 2008, that stimulated a good deal of clinical and research interest in the field of burden of care in psychiatry. We were pleased to provide advice and assistance to several research groups nationally and internationally to get involved in such an important aspect of psychiatric care. However, one of the related aspects of family burden of care, the economics of care-giving, continues to be lacking. The complexity of the concept and many of its components that defy accurate counting may have discouraged some researchers from investigating such an important concept. While it's possible to cost tangible components of family expenses, such as housing, food, etc., it is rather difficult to put a monetary value on psychological and emotional issues, such as distress, feelings of loss, low self-esteem, stigma and absence of a productive, self-fulfilling role. It is erroneous to cost burden of care among the intangibles simply as a result of lack of methodology. It is clear that the analysis of health costs needs to be grounded in a clear understanding of clinical reality. Clinicians need to be familiar with health economic concepts and be able to generate reliable clinical data that can be useful in cost analysis. A reliable economic evaluation of the costs of family care and the benefits of family interventions is not only important for policy making, but also for negotiating support, reimbursement and compensation to caregivers.

So far, a number of broad strategies have been developed to ease the burden of family care, but many such approaches have not been fully researched nor has their value been confirmed. Among the promising recent approaches, the provision of legally mandated "community-based treatment orders" may prove helpful in eliminating some of the needs for urgent hospitalizations and frequent hospitalizations. It would be interesting to see how effective this approach has been, for both patients and caregivers, in the few countries where it has been introduced.

Obviously, a well informed and balanced advocacy, as well as minimizing the impact of stigma, and improving the effectiveness and quality of psychiatric care can prove to be helpful for families, patients and society at large.

The Society

• Cost of Mental Disorders

The staggering cost of mental disorders, both direct and indirect, has been extensively documented in several studies, including those reported by Professor Martin Knapp and others from the London School of Economics. Unaddressed or poorly-addressed mental health issues can negatively impact serious social concerns, apart from the monetary costs. It is frequently difficult to assign a cost for emotional and psychological sufferings inherent to the struggle with major psychiatric disorders, such as schizophrenia or severe depression. Social isolation, stigma, loss of productivity and poverty all frequently lead to long-term disabilities. And that is where the major challenges are with the current schemes of compensation for psychiatric disabilities. Fortunately, the majority of western societies are morally committed and judged by their ability to take care of their disabled citizens, including those with psychiatric disabilities. However, the major challenges in such variable compensation schemes have been how closely these schemes are tied and coordinated with clear clinical recovery plans.

Generally, the most optimum scheme is the one that is successfully integrated with clinical management and care plans. That is where many disability compensation plans tend to fail, leaving the disabled person with nothing or little to do, lacking interest or a means of deriving pleasure or any feelings of fulfillment from their life. The assumption that psychiatrically disabled persons are not capable of making a contribution is wrong most of the time. Otherwise, we are contributing to a state of more hopelessness and dependence. The models of disabilities compensation need to be revisited, as there needs to be a positive balance, not only by recognizing the limitations, but also empowering recipients to share some responsibility in the process of their own recovery. We do not need to go back to what was billed in the past as moral work therapy, while in fact it was unethical and coercive exploitation. We need to reform the process to make it a desirable option, grounded in a clear ethical framework. Obviously, that is a cost that can contribute to minimizing disabilities and inequities, by providing more opportunities.

- **Bill C-7 and the expansion of the right to Medical Assistance in Dying**

Another more recent challenge to psychiatry has been the introduction by the Canadian government of what is known as Bill C-7, which expands the right to medical assistance in dying, to include psychiatric disorders. By modifying the law and removing the clause that required the patients' death to be "reasonably foreseeable", the newly introduced bill will certainly undermine the rights of disabled persons and make it more likely to accept assisted suicide, rather than be properly and effectively treated and supported. And this is the serious concern in broadening the concept to include psychiatric conditions. No question or any argument about how serious and devastating some psychiatric conditions, like severe non-remittent, long term depression or losing the self in chronic psychotic states can be. The ethical question that clearly arises is how effective or appropriate are psychiatric treatments? As already mentioned, I do believe that psychiatric treatments, whether medications or various types of therapy, are generally documented as minimally- or non-effective at all. I am afraid that by opening the door to assisted dying, misuse and abuse is unpreventable. Instead of assisting severe sufferers of psychiatric disorders to die, the major emphasis has to be how to improve the failing psychiatric treatments and how to make them more effective and relevant. It is a moral and ethical challenge that psychiatry needs to confront, before opening the door to assisted dying.

• Lack of Integration with other Medical Specialities

Another societal gap has been the lack of integration or the presence of psychiatry as a permanent member of family-practice medical teams. The concept has proven to be successful where it has been implemented. It has not only managed to cut down referral waiting times to see a psychiatrist, but has also provided much better integrated care. The excuse to not integrate psychiatry has often been lack of funding, which is short-sighted if one recognizes its eventual cost benefits. The complicating problem is frequently due to the fragmentation in health care plans and budgets, that put family medicine and psychiatry in different administrative and budgetary pockets.

• Medicalizing Everyday Conflicts

Another societal concern has been the trend to medicalize everyday conflicts into medical or psychiatric problems, that then acquire a title and require medications or psycho-therapeutic approaches that crop up in no time. The neurasthenia of the past has morphed into *chronic fatigue syndrome* or *fibromyalgia*, with endless investigations and treatments, but with little real benefit. The past challenging cases of "hysteria" that flooded psychoanalytic practices in the past has migrated to outpatient clinics of *functional neurology,* after psychoanalysts lost interest in its treatment. Shyness, which is a human trait, has become a diagnostic disorder that requires vigorous treatments, and so on. The widespread use of the diagnosis of "post-traumatic stress disorder", without a discerning and clear definition, has made it a popular diagnostic condition, no different than the "flu" in medical practice. Falling into these fads and trends tends to dilute energy and time for attending to more serious concerns, and creates a poor image of psychiatry as the treatment for all societal aches and pains.

I do believe that adequately dealing with serious mental health issues is not only the domain for individual citizens, but also equally important for the society as a whole, in terms of ensuring some coherence, tolerance and ability to handle national threats and crises.

The Imperative of the Search for a New Psychiatry

Psychiatry as a medical specialty is focused on disorders of the brain and behaviour. In contrast, unlike many other medical specialties, psychiatry deals with the totality of the person. For a cardiologist the person is mostly a heart and an intricate system of vasculature. For a nephrologist, the body is more about kidneys and a system that deals with getting rid of metabolites and end-products. In psychiatry, dealing with the totality of the person is reflected in a complicated set of behaviour mediated and tightly orchestrated centrally by the brain, with major inputs from the environment, both internal and external, certainly a major challenge. A psychiatric assessment not only draws on information from neurosciences, but also from other vast sources of human experiences, like sociology, psychology, history and philosophy, as well as an endless world of subjective impressions and experiences.

What distinguishes a psychiatrist from many others who may have access to some of the same sources of knowledge and information, is the detailed study and knowledge of the neuroscience of brain functioning, which is what a psychiatrist is frequently unable to clearly project. Admittedly, we do not have the complete knowledge that can guide us to more firm conclusions, but the incomplete information we do have can still prove powerful in amplifying the message and enhancing its impact, and only if we are able to master such knowledge and recognize its value and its limitations. In short, I do strongly believe that what is lacking in psychiatry is science, a strong science that can empower psychiatry. That is why psychiatry is lagging behind several other medical specialties.

As I am writing this last chapter of the book, a major science breakthrough has been announced regarding the international scientific development of a Covid-19 vaccine in less than a year, a project that usually takes several years. It is an amazing scientific feat and demonstration of what pooling international expertise and resources can accomplish. Taking schizophrenia as the ultimate example of a century of mostly failed brain research, the counter argument has often been that the brain is far more complex. True, schizophrenia is not going to be resolved in one year, but it requires a plan and international collaboration like the one behind the Covid-19 vaccine, which is built on an established strong foundation of basic sciences. If it could be done in a complex field like immunology, sure it could be done with schizophrenia or bipolar mood disorders.

Besides research and its many gaps and inadequacies, psychiatry, as practiced these days, is failing many, including patients and their families, their doctors and society at large, as outlined in previous chapters. That clearly means that the status quo is not acceptable anymore. In reaching such a sad conclusion, as formulated in this book, my decision in advance has been not to quickly jump into the trap of creating a long list or an over-inclusive "manifesto" of proposed reforms. Pointing to deficits and areas of failure is one thing, constructing a list of reforms or corrections is another matter, that can only be reached after extensive discussions and consensus by all the stakeholders. Patients, their families, their doctors, decision-makers and those who take care of the financial purse, as well as many others who are concerned, including me, also you, the readers of this book, need to be represented around the table. The final product should be an evolution of new thinking turned into a tidy, practical, affordable, clearly understood and field-tested approach. The hope in going through the challenges of composing this book is more to stimulate a dialogue that can usher in an exhaustive, but very focused process, that eventually can lead to a broad consensus in principle. Obviously, implementation needs to be shaped by the unique characteristics of every region within the national guiding principles.

The question that I still repeatedly ask myself, is why do I think this plan has more of a chance of success, when many similar plans in the past have failed? The reason for my current optimism is that the level of dissatisfaction by so many of those involved in psychiatric care, such as the recipients and providers, has reached a high-level of concern regarding the future of psychiatry. When dissatisfaction of poor psychiatric care continues for a long time, serious things can and do happen. By necessity, people either will continue to use an inadequate system, getting from it whatever they can, but at the same time they lose hope and trust in psychiatry, that slowly lead to isolation and further decline. A much better outcome is to face psychiatry's shortcomings and embark on a meaningful and realistic reforms that can save and strengthen psychiatry's scientific and human core. And that is my sincere hope.

Postscript

The Pleasure and Perils of Academia A
Few Reflections on Academic Life

One of my career ambitions as a medical student in the early 1950s, was to become an academician. I am delighted and feeling fortunate that such a deep desire has been accomplished, through perseverance, hard work and taking risks, as well as through accidental and unplanned happenings, both pleasant and, at times, as an obstacle or a distraction.

As I completed the manuscript for this book, introducing some of my academic contributions, I acutely realized that though I spent almost my professional life in academia, I never reflected purposefully on my feelings about academic life and touching upon its pleasures and perils. At the beginning of my career, the modus operandi at that time of academia was captured by the rather humorous statement "publish or perish". Amassing a respectable list of publications, strengthened by recommendations of being a good teacher or being reliable in serving university affairs, was often enough to climb the academic ladder. The challenge, at that time, was how to get published in the relatively few, but well-known journals. It also depended not only on the quality of science, but also on the politics and which scientific group one belonged to, as well as the expertise, or lack of it, of the chosen peer reviewers. Nevertheless, it was mostly a straight-forward and somewhat predictable process. But, then, as frequently happens in life, changes crept in, and usually in slow motion. More educated populations, more academic expansions and more technological advances meant more aspirants for academic careers, all competing for limited publishing space. By the 1990s, the academic motto had become "...you can publish but still perish". The game had changed and its requirements were expanded to include raising external funds or seeking endowments. Meanwhile, there was a massive proliferation in the number of journals that claimed to be rigorous and scientific, plus there was the rise in electronic self-publications that made the field of publishing look like a jungle. A sweeping glance at the massive amount of available information proved to be disquieting, since a good chunk of what was being published was not science or, at best, was at the edge of science and just mere repetition. Relying only on information from the standard and well-established sources proved also to be uncertain, as it was not free from bias, which has been demonstrated in recent years by the rise in the number of corrections or recalls of already published data. Sadly, instances of plagiarism and litigation have been on the rise. Even the scientific language, itself, has become more confrontational and less civil. The fierce competition and the rush to publish are becoming a threat to the fabric of scientific truth. I recognize the thrill of being first to publish, as well as the hefty rewards in leading to notoriety or patents. Is that an early sign of academic decline, perpetuated by its own moments of great success?

Competition among scientists and in between academic institutions is a healthy matter for the advancement of science, but are we turning it quickly into a fish market? Certainly, it is a serious note of concern for the future. As for dealing with the massive amount of available information churned up by the extensive number of new journals, there is no need nor a way to control its quality, except for the readers to develop something like a crude "facts sieve" to sort through the information, which can be aided by opinion leaders' commentaries. I recall many years back, in the 1970s, when I was working at my first job in Canada, at the University of Toronto, in the Department of Pharmacology, I naively asked my boss and mentor, Professor E. Sellers about the problem of scientific journals being filled with publications that seemed to me, at that time, to be irrelevant and lacking any value. He told me that in science, if 5% of what gets published withstands the test of time, it would be a reasonable cost outcome.

On balance, academic life can be enjoyable and thrilling. It can confer some control of one's own time and provide the opportunity to explore other human endeavours, as well as broaden one's professional, social and personal contacts, that can facilitate collaboration. It can also take one to different unusual places or events that one would most likely not have considered. I still vividly recall a number of such places, events and people that I encountered through my academic engagements.

An academic visit in 1984 to Spandau, the old psychiatric hospital in Berlin, just a few years before the collapse of the Berlin Wall, I was able to have a glimpse at East Berliners climbing a ladder over the wall, which, in reality, was the fence of the ancient psychiatric hospital. On another occasion, on the other side of the world, I made an academic visit to a small psychiatric hospital where Professor Flor-Henry conducted his well-known neuropsychiatric research, situated in the small town of Penoka, Alberta, in Canada, on the highway between the cities of Calgary and Edmonton. The visit gave me the very exciting opportunity of having truckers join my lecture at the local truck stop, following a dinner there, arranged by the psychiatric staff in Ponoka. Apparently, that was the only place in that small town that had a decent restaurant to invite visitors. As my slides started rolling on the make-shift screen of white bed sheets, truckers joined in and participated fully in the comments and questions. It was an eye-opener for me, confirming my belief about the need for psychiatry to go to the people, rather than waiting for the people to come to it.

At another academic event, in the Ice Hotel outside the small town of Kiruna, in Sweden, about 300 kilometres above the arctic circle, I shared a chalet with Professor John Waddington, from Ireland, who was also a speaker at the annual meeting of the Irish Psychiatric Association. The Ice Hotel structure, built from blocks of ice, was a remarkably creative engineering feat, with all of the furniture, utensils and art objects also made of ice. The temperature outside was close to 35 degrees below zero, and only a pleasant one or two degrees indoors. Based on my past Moscow experiences, I carried with me a stock of warm clothes, including very warm socks. I lent a pair to John, as his socks proved to be inadequate, and since then, every time I saw John at the Davos meeting, we shared an inside joke about my travelling socks.

An academic visit to the Department of Psychiatry at Fudan University in Shanghai, China, was a unique opportunity and in many ways another eye-opener. Not only was the department impressive by its size and the population it serves, but also by how many of the academic staff spoke good English, which certainly facilitated my visit. Nevertheless, my presentations were neatly translated into Mandarine in advance and presented side-by-side with the English version. On any given working day, there were thirty psychiatrists running the outpatient clinic, which functioned as a drop-in clinic, without advance appointments. It drew patients from the vast territory of Shanghai, which itself had a population of over twenty-five million. The large city was divided into several health districts and each district had its full team of psychiatric care, side-by-side with other health teams. I was fortunate that my visit included a meeting with one psychiatric screening team that takes care of all school students from early grades to completion of their school studies. It is a massive, but very important undertaking in the early detection of mental and family health issues, which is an excellent idea that needs to be replicated in every large western city.

Another remarkable event at the conclusion of the annual Lundeck symposium in Copenhagen, speakers were invited to a private dinner hosted by Lundbeck's president, Mr. Petersen, in his house in a suburb outside Copenhagen. The dinner was a celebration of the famous Danish writer Isak Denisen, whose real name was Karin Plexin. The dinner was organized on the theme of one of her well-known books, "Babette's Feast". It included twelve exotic courses, each preceded by a different wine and a short poem or literary quotation from her book.

The dinner extended to the early hours of the morning and included an impressive review of several Eskimo art objects, collected by the host while serving as president of a mining company in Iceland, during his frequent visits to a Canadian arctic town on Baffin Island. This initiated a lively conversation about Eskimo culture and the role of culture, generally, in influencing the expression of mental illness. At the end of the dinner every guest was given an English translation of the book, as well as a video of the film that was based on the book.

One of my early contacts in Vienna, in 1984, was Professor Wolfgang Gaebel, while the two of us were participating in a conference there. This has led to a long-lasting friendship and collaboration that has extended from Berlin, where he was then located, and later to Dusseldorf. It was in Dusseldorf that we mounted our collaborative program concerning prediction research in psychiatry, which started with an international conference and culminated in a book with the same title. I recall having to lock myself in the nurses' residence of his hospital in Dusseldorf for few days, to complete the book manuscript in order to meet the deadline.

In Denmark, I had the unique opportunity to visit St. Hans Psychiatric Hospital, some thirty kilometres outside of Copenhagen, arranged by Professor Les Gerlach, who was one of my early supporters in my struggle to establish the science of the concept of "subjective tolerability" to antipsychotic medications, against all the doubters who labelled it as "soft science". St. Hans is one of the oldest psychiatric facilities in Europe and well-known for its impressive program of psychiatric rehabilitation, including equally impressive occupational and art therapy programs. Indeed, at the end of my visit to the art therapy studios and the unique psychiatry museum, I was given as a gift a nice picture composed by a patient, which is still hanging in my office among other patients' creative art objects (a copy is shown). It was memorable after the impressive visit to St. Hans, to have the opportunity to have lunch and meet Mrs. Wensch Gerlach, in their beautiful house, which reflected not only their

Danish fine art taste, but also their generosity and kindness, that I continue to remember warmly.

A collage based on traditional Danish folklore (artwork on paper 12" x 18"), by patients attending an art therapy session at St. Hans Hospital in Denmark
(Presented to the author, A.G. Awad, at the end
of an academic visit to the hospital.)

Reflecting back on all my years as an academician, it certainly was and still continues to be an exceptional learning experience that has no end. It can be thrilling, but also at times equally frustrating. For academics, one has to be equipped and well-prepared for it, as well as being deeply bound and committed to a real interest in genuine search for truth and scientific facts. Otherwise, lacking any of these gifts and commitments, academia can be dull, frustrating and a total waste, leading only to a dead end. In simple conclusion, my academic life has been enriched by the many contacts I've enjoyed, cherished and will always value.

PART X

Conclusion

Conclusion

As I completed the manuscript for this book, two observations became clear. The first observation has been the realization that my seventy years of professional and academic career has, for the most part, corresponded with the development of the new era of modern psychiatry that had its beginnings in the late 1940s. The other observation has been how the contents of the manuscript naturally fell into two distinct parts that are closely connected. The early part tells the story of my training across three continents, in Cairo, Moscow, Rome and Toronto, followed by over fifty years of practice in Toronto as an academic psychiatrist and clinical neuroscientist. The latter part of the manuscript provides a critical analysis of the current state of psychiatric practices, which receives a failing grade. It is almost as if I had to prove my professional and academic credentials before delivering my negative verdict, regarding the failing state of current psychiatric practices.

In Cairo, I developed a clear antipathy to psychiatry as a medical student, following my observation of a session of "insulin coma therapy", which looked barbaric and inhumane. A few years later, practicing as a rural physician in a remote region of Egypt, I successfully confronted endemic pellagra and pellagra madness, that gave me the first inkling of any interest in the neurosciences. Gaining knowledge about the ancient history of the development of one of the earliest concepts of the mental asylum in eighth-century Cairo, broadened my interest in connecting modern history with the ancient past. I came to realize how colonial authorities in Egypt may have introduced better organization and management of the mental asylum, but, unfortunately, colonial psychiatry had deliberately delayed the development of academic psychiatry in Cairo for self-serving reasons. Meanwhile, the evolving transformational developments emanating from France, Canada and the United States ushered in the development and introduction of the first antipsychotic chlorpromazine and drastically changed the face and practice of psychiatry, as well as bolstered the role of the psychiatrist as a medical specialist.

In Moscow, focusing on the study of the concept of "stress" and its relevance to health and illnesses, I had to confront a range of challenging issues that dealt with politics, ideology, loneliness and love. Living in a formally declared atheist society, forced me, in spite of my neutral stand about religion, to think seriously about the highly debated question of whether sciences can flourish in the absence of religion. They can.

Returning to Cairo after completing my studies proved to be a major disappointment, which followed my mis-appointment. Being posted in a highly sensitive senior position and overseeing the urgent toxicological studies of the weekly imported grains arriving at the Port of Alexandria, put me face to face with inherent corruption, dirty politics and bad science, and it surely did not require a PhD scientist. Saved by being awarded a post-doctoral year of fellowship at one of the best health research institutes in Rome, consolidated my academic interests in the concept of "stress" and, more importantly, it gave me the opportunity to avoid returning to Cairo, as well as the freedom to choose my own career and destiny.

Unplanned and unconsidered, I found myself accepting an academic post in the newly opened medical school at the University of Calgary, in Alberta, Canada. A stop-over in Toronto for a few days, en-route to Calgary, mysteriously lasted for the next fifty years, as a result of an unexpected nor planned offer from the Department of Pharmacology at the University of Toronto. Two years after the successful publication of my first co-authored article in the medical journal The Lancet, I moved to psychiatry, which became my clinical home-base, where my neuroscience background and psychiatry finally came together.

The next fifty years in Toronto proved to be a truly successful academic story with its many accomplishments, planned and accidental, its disappointments and missed opportunities. Early on, my academic focus centred on schizophrenia and the needs of the person behind the illness. Issues like quality of care, quality of life, wellness and patient-centred care became topics of our research programs. My quest to understand why a number of persons with schizophrenia hated to take their antipsychotic medication became a thirty years of a dogged research project, before its neurobiological basis was clarified in a definitive neuroimaging study for the first time. A new science, then, was born: the science of subject tolerability, that slowly evolved into a major element in drug response, as well as the genesis of the development of comorbid drug addictive behaviour.

The important second part of the book, the analysis of the current state of psychiatric practice, proved that the post-chlorpromazine peak of progress did not proceed linearly, as was expected. A few brief peaks of hope and optimism were separated by rather lengthy stagnant periods with little or no progress and increasing disappointments and frustrations. Psychiatric treatments, whether medications or psychotherapy, continued to be at best only partially or non-effective, and medications also continued to carry an unacceptable range of serious side-effects, as well as having to be taken almost life long.

Psychotherapy, as the second important arm of psychiatric treatments, proved to be in a state of chaos, with more than four hundred types or approaches in existence, the most of which were never validated nor based on a reasonable conceptual framework. Psychotherapy is lengthy and costly, which limits its accessibility and also poses issues of equity and equality among professionals. Such serious issues of accessibility, competence, equity and equality forces the question of whether psychotherapy, in view of its importance, needs to stand as an independent discipline associated with psychiatry, but regulated on its own by the development of a professional academy, provincial boards or a college. Such developments can ensure qualifications and expertise, as well as maintenance of competence and the development of a strong academic base.

The lack of any etiological breakthroughs of major psychiatric disorders, such as schizophrenia or manic depression, clearly points to a fundamental lack of theory, the right theory and also to misdirected searches, complicated by mostly invalidated and artificially constructed classificatory systems. The role of the psychiatrist is continually being eroded by pressures from other professionals demanding a bigger share of psychiatric services, as well as a wide range of unmet science and service needs. Such pressures tend to leave the psychiatrist not feeling strongly backed by science, and burdened by service demands in clearly fragmented service models.

The lack of an adequate and updated psychiatric training curricula fails to prepare psychiatrists for future challenges. Many training curricula continue to be embedded by old and antiquated theories and concepts. The disappearance of adequate neurology training in many psychiatric curricula has left numerous psychiatrists unable to follow advances in neurosciences. It has also led to further splintering by neurology recently carving the new subspecialty of behavioural neurology, which is somewhat equivalent to our forgotten neuropsychiatry. Hopefully, through experts' pressure on both sides pressing for a merger between the two subspecialties to consolidate expertise and resources, a third discipline may arise besides psychiatry and neurology and becomes more focused on the core of neurosciences.

The cost of psychiatric disorders has been adequately documented as high, in both monetary terms as well as in personal sufferings and family impacts, several task forces with high level commissions have failed to provide more than tweaks or minor improvements, which have not satisfied consumers nor service providers. Adding more funds, as frequently cried for, has little chance of improving a broken system, which requires radical realignments of services that would benefit from new thinking of different strategies and grounded in a strong foundation of neuroscience and psychosocial sciences. Evolving new knowledge in physics, mathematics, computer and communication sciences, artificial intelligence, ethicists and medical philosophers need to be added to research teams. Similarly, a change in science and opinion leaders as well as influencers who tend to perpetuate the current status quo, may become necessary and required at times.

Psychiatry is clearly failing many: the patients, their families, their doctors and the society at large. The time is now, to search for a new psychiatry, before psychiatry completely loses the trust and confidence of patients and families, and burden more doctors. Equally serious, it can turn psychiatry into a second- or even third-class medical specialty, that fails to attract the best candidates and is left desperately struggling to secure a respected and more effective place among various medical specialties.

SELECTED BIBLIOGRAPHY

Part I: The Cairo University Years

Hager Thomas. Ten Drugs: How Plants, Powders and Pills Have Shaped the History of Modern Medicine. Abrams Publishing, 2019

Tignor Robert. Modernization of British Colonial Rule in Egypt; 1882 – 1914. Princeton Legacy Library, 2016

Doroshow Deborah. Performing a Cure for Schizophrenia: Insulin Coma Therapy on the Wards. Journal of the History of Medicine and Allied Service, 2007, 62:213-243

Keller Richard. Madness and Colonization: Psychiatry in the British and French Empires 1800 – 1962. Oxford University Press, 2001

Rotman, Salma. Egypt From Independence to Revolution, 1919 – 1952. Syracuse University Press, 1991

Mitchel Timothy. Colonizing Egypt. Cambridge University Press, 1988

Kamil, Jill. Coptic Egypt, History and Guide. American University in Cairo Press, 1987

Carter BL. The Copts in Egyptian Politics 1918 – 1952. The American University in Cairo Press, 1986

Ansari Hamied. Egypt, the Stalled Society. The American University in Cairo Press, 1986

Foucault Michel. Madness and Civilization: A History of Insanity in the Age of Reason. Vintage Books, 1961

Kline Nathan S (editor). Psychopharmacology Frontiers, The Second International Congress of Psychiatry and Psychopharmacology Symposium. Little, Brown and Company, 1957

Part II: My First Job – The Bani Ayoub Years (1958 – 1961)

Blease CR, Colloca L, Kaptchuk TJ. Are Open-Label Placebos Ethical? Informed Consent and Ethical Equivocations. Bioethics, 2016, 30:407-414

Schedlowski M et al. Neuro-Bio-Behavioral Mechanisms of Placebo and Nocebo, Implications for Clinical Trials and Clinical Practice. Pharmacological Review, 2015, 67:697-731

Jarow Gail. Red Madness: How a Medical Mystery Changed What We Eat. Calkins Creek, 2015

Hegyi J et al. Dermatitis, Dementia and Diarrhea. International Journal of Dermatology, 2004, 43:1-5

Veatch Robert. Experimental Pregnancy. Hastings Center Report, 1971, 1:265-270

Goldzieher J et al. A Placebo-Controlled Double Blind Crossover Investigation to the Side Effects Attributed to Oral Contraceptives. Fertility and Sterility, 1971, 22:600-623

Goldzieher J et al. Nervousness and Depression Attributed to Oral Contraceptives: A Double-Blind Placebo-Controlled Study. American Journal of Obstetrics and Gynecology, 1971, 111:1013-1020

Sydenstricher VP. History of Pellagra, Its Recognition and Its Conquest. American Journal of Clinical Nutrition, 1958, 6:400-416

Pepper OH Perry. A Note on the Placebo. American Journal of Pharmacy, 1945, 117:409-412

Goldberger Joseph, Wheeler GA. Experimental Pellagra in the Human Subjects Brought about by a Restricted Diet. Public Health Reports 1915, 30:3336-3339

Part III: My Moscow Years (1961-1964)

Zubovitch Gene. Russia's Journey From Orthodoxy to Atheism and Back Again. Danforth Centre in Religion and Politics, Washington University at St. Louise, 2018

Stepaniants M, Johnson J. Regional and Identity in Modern Russia, The Revival of Orthodoxy and Islam. Routledge Publishing, 2016

Melnichenko GA et al. On the History of Endocrinology in Russia. Problems of Endocrinology 2012, 58:74-76 (in Russian)

Fox Michael David. Religion, Science and Political Religion in the Soviet Context. Cambridge University Press, 2011

Krementsov N. Hormones and Bolsheviks: From Organotherapy to Experimental Endocrinology, History of Science Society. The University of Chicago Press, 2008

Borrell-Carrio F et al. The Biopsychosocial Model Twenty-Five Years Later, Principles, Practice and Scientific Inquiry. Annals of Family Medicine, 2004, 2:576-582

Levitan Carl. Russian Church and Scientists Lay Revolutionary Quarrels to Rest. Nature, March 26, 1998

Engel George L. The Clinical Application of Biopsychosocial Model. American Journal of Psychiatry, 1980, 137:535-544

Engel George L. The Need for a New Medical Model: A Challenge for Biomedicine. Science 1977, 196:129-136

Awad AG, Shedrina KN. On the Nature of the Blocking Effect of Desoxycorticosterone on Adrenotrophic Function of the Hypothesis. Problems of Endocrinology and Hormone Therapy, 1965, 612:433-451 (in Russian)

Awad AG. A Comparative Study of the Blocking Effects of Corticosteroids on the Pituitary/Adrenal Asix of the Adult Animals Relative to Experimental Stress. Dissertation for the Degree of "Candidate in Medical Sciences", 1964

Selye Hans. Stress and the General Adaptation Syndrome. British Medical Journal, 1950, 17:1383-1392

Selye Hans. The General Adaptation Syndrome and the Diseases of Adaptation. Journal of Clinical Endocrinology, 1946, 6:119-131

Canon Walter B. The Role of Emotion in Disease. Annals of Internal Medicine, 1936, 9:1453-1465

Part IV: Back to Cairo (1964-1968)

Walsh, Declan. Egypt's Population Hits 100 Million – Celebration is Muted. New York Times, March 9, 2021

Scobie Grant M. Government Policy and Food Imports: The Case of Wheat in Egypt. International Food Policy Research Institute – Research Report 29, 1981

How did Egypt become the largest importer of wheat in the world. Quora.com, www.quora.com, 1978

Part V: The Post-Doctoral Year in Rome (1968)

De Castro Pablo, Marsili Daniela, Modigliani Sara. Storia e Identita de Une Ente Di Recerca L'Instituto Superiore Di Sanita Attraverso Racconti et Testimonianse Orali. ISDS Publications Roma, 2011

Cartoni C, Awad AG, Carpi A. Effects of Aldosterone, Dexamethasone and Corticosterone on the Cardiovascular Reactivity of Adrenalectomized Rate. Archive International of Pharmacodynamics and Therapy, 1969, 182:98-111

Barzini Luigi. L'Italiene (The Italians). Thrift Books, 1964

Interlude and Part VI: The Final Stop – Toronto, Canada (1969)

Park Seon-Cheol. Karl Jaspers: 100 Years of General Psychopathology (Algemeine Pathologie) – Implications for Current Psychiatry. Psychiatric Investigation, 2019, 16:99-108

A. George Awad. Revisiting the Concept of Subjective Tolerability to Antipsychotic Medications in Schizophrenia and Its Clinical and Research Implications: Thirty Years Later. CNS Drugs, 2019, 33:1-8

Abrams A. The Neuroscience of Creativity. Cambridge University, Cambridge University Press, 2018

Preedy V. (editor). Neuropathology of Drug Addictions and Substance Misuse, Volume 1, 2016, Elsevier Inc.

A. George Awad. The Neurobiology of Comorbid Drug Abuse in Schizophrenia and Psychotic Disorders, in: Victor Preedy (editor), Neuropathology of Drug Addictions and Substance Misuse., Volume 1, Elsevier Inc., 2016:82-88

Hafner Heinz. Descriptive Psychiatry, Phenomenology and the Legacy of Karl Jaspers. Dialogues in Clinical Neurosciences, 2015, 17:19-29

A. George Awad. The Patient: At the Centre of "Patient-Reported Outcomes". Expert Review of Pharmacoeconomics and Outcomes Research, 2015, 15:29-31

A. George Awad, LNP Voruganti. Revisiting the Self-Medication Hypothesis in Light of the New Data Linking Low Striatal Dopamine to Comorbid Addictive Behaviour. Therapeutic Advances in Psychopharmacology, 2015, 3:172-178

A. George Awad. Is It Time to Consider Comorbid Substance Abuse as a New Indication for Antipsychotic Drug Development. Journal of Psychopharmacology, 2012, 26:953-957

Barc Agatha. The History of Lakeshore Psychiatric Hospital in Toronto, 2011: blogto.com/city/2011/04/a brief history of Lakeshore Psychiatric Hospital

Barc Agatha. The History of the Toronto Lunatic Asylum. blogto/com/city/2011/04/nostalgia_tripping_lunatic_asylum, 2011

Andreason Nancy. DSM and the Death of Phenomenology in America, An Example of Unintended Consequences. Schizophrenia Bulletin, 2007, 33:108-112

Voruganti LNP, Awad AG. Sbujective and Behavioural Consequences of Striatal Dopamine Depletion in Schizophrenia: Findings From In Vivo SPECT Study. Schizophrenia Research, 2006, 88:179-186

Awad AG, Voruganti LNP. Neuroleptic Dysphoria, Comorbid Drug Abuse in Schizophrenia and the Emerging Science of Subjective Tolerability – Towards a New Synthesis. Journal of Dual Diagnosis, 2005, 1:83-93

Voruganti LNP, Awad AG. Neuroleptic Dysphoria: Towards a New Synthesis. Psychopharmacology, 2004, 171:121-132

Awad AG, Voruganti LNP. The Subjective/Objective Dichotomy in Schizophrenia from Dysphoria to Striatal Dopamine Receptors. Schizophrenia Bulletin, 2002, 53:199-200

Awad AG, Voruganti LNP. The Subjective/Objective Dichotomy: Implications for Nosology, Treatment and Research, (editor) W. Gaebel Zukunfts – Perspektiven in Psychiatrie und Psychotherapie. Steinkopff, Darmstadt, Germany, 2002, pp 21-27

Awad AG. The Psychology of Medication-Taking: The Development of a Research program in Psychopharmacology, in: Ban TA, Healy D, Shorter E (editors). From Psychopharmacology to Neurosycho Pharmacology in 1980s and the Story of CAMP, as Told in Autobiography. Budapest: Animula Publishing House, 2002, 130-134

MacDonald Donald Cameron. The Happy Warrior, Political Memoirs, 2nd Edition. Dundurn Press, Toronto, Canada, 1998

Awad AG. Subjective Response to Neuroleptics in Schizophrenia. Schizophrenia Bulletin, 1993, 19:609-617

A. George Awad. Methodological and Design Issues in Clinical Trials of New Neuroleptics: An Overview. British Journal of Psychiatry, 1993, 163 (suppl. 22):51-57

Awad AG. Drug Therapy in Schizophrenia – Variability of the Outcome and Prediction of Response. Canadian Journal of Psychiatry, 1989, 34:711-720

Awad AG. Do We Need New Antidepressants? Annals of The Royal College of Physicians & Surgeons, 1985, 18:333-338

Hogan TP, Awad AG. Pharmacotherapy and Suicide in Schizophrenia. Canadian Journal of Psychiatry, 1983, 28:277-281

Pirsig Robert. Zen and the Art of Motorcycle Maintenance. Bantom Books New York, 1976

Sellers EM, Awad AG, Schonbaum E. Long-acting Thyroid Stimulator in Graves Disease. The Lancet, 1970, 296:335-338

Part VII: Quality of Care in Psychiatry

Awad A. George. The Concept of Quality of Life: Schizophrenia from an "Ethereal Entity" to a Valued Health Outcome. Journal of Psychosocial Rehabilitation and Mental Health (editorial), 2016, 3:51-52

Awad AG. New Antipsychotics: Compliance, Quality of Life and Subjective Tolerability – Are Patients Better Off? Canadian Journal of Psychiatry, 2004, 49:297-302

Awad A. George, Voruganti LNP, Heselgrave R. Measuring Quality of Life in Patients with Schizophrenia. Pharmacoeconomics, 1997, 11:32-47

Awad AG, Darby P, Garfinkel P. Psychopharmacology Training in Psychiatric Residency Programs - "The Canadian Scene". Canadian Journal of Psychiatry, 1991, 36:21-25

Awad AG. Measurement of Quality of Care in Mental Health Services; Is it Possible? Quality Assurance Quarterly, 1986, 2:12-16

Smits HI. The PSRO in Perspective. New England Journal of Medicine, 1981, 30:305-309

Awad AG, Durost HB, MacCormick W. Evaluation of Quality of Care in Psychiatry. Pergamon Press, 1980

Goran MJ. The Evaluation of the PSRO Hospital Review System. Medical Care, 1979, 17 (suppl. 5):1-47

Part VIII: Psychiatric Outcomes

Awad A. George. The Concept of Wellness in Psychiatric and Substance-Use Disorders, in: Waguih E, IsHak W (editor), The Handbook of Wellness, Cambridge University Press, 2020

Awad AG, Voruganti LNP. The Impact of Newer Atypical Antipsychotics on Patient-Reported Outcomes in Schizophrenia. CNS Drugs, 2013, 27:625-635

Voruganti LNP, Awad AG et al. Cost Utility Analysis in Schizophrenia – A feasibility Study. Pharmacoeconomics, 2000, 17:273-286

Awad AG, Voruganti LNP. Cost Utility Analysis in Schizophrenia. Journal of Clinical Psychiatry, 1999, (Suppl. 3):22-29

Gerteis Margaret, Edgman-Levitan Susan, Daley Jennifer, Delbanco Thomas L. (eds). Through the Patient's Eyes: Understanding and Promoting Patient-Centered Care. Jossey-Bass Inc., Publishers, 1993

Greenfield S, Kaplan SH, Ware JE, Jr. Expanding Patient Involvement in Care: Effects on Patient Outcome. Annals of Internal Medicine, 1985, 102:520-528

Brady DS. The Patient's Role in Clinical Decision-Making. Annals of Internal Medicine, 1980, 93:718-722

Part IX: Current Psychiatric Practices

Gaind Sonu. MAID (Medical Assistance in Dying) for Mental Illness is Grave Discrimination. An Opinion. The Toronto Star, March 2, 2021

Reinhardt Uwe. Priced Out: The Economic and Ethical Costs of American Health Care. Princeton University Press, 2020

Bourgeois James et al. Psychiatry of the Future – 2030 and Beyond. Journal of Psychiatry Reform, 2020. journalofpsychiatryreform.com/2020/07/271/psychiatry_of_the_future_2030_and_beyond

Heike Gerger et al. What Are the Key Characteristics of a "Good" Psychotherapy? Calling for Ethical Patient Involvement. Front. Psychiatry.02June2020/https://doi.org/10.3389/fpsy2020.00406

Harrington Anne. Mind Fixers – Psychiatry's Troubled Search for the Biology of Mental Illness, 2019, W.W. Norton & Company

Groopman Jerome. The Troubled History of Psychiatry. The New Yorker, May 20, 2019

Haelle Tara. A Neurology and Psychiatry Merger: Quest for the Inevitable. Neurology Advisor, February 11, 2019

Eppel Alan et al. Should Psychiatrists Practice Psychotherapy. Journal of Psychiatry Reform, 2019. journalofpsychiatryreform.com/2019/04/14/should_psychiatrists_practice_psychotherapy

Deans Emily. A Roadmap for the Future of Psychiatry and It's Not the DSM.5. Psychology Today, June 1, 2017

Bhurga Denesh et al. The WPA-Lancet Psychiatry Commission on the Future of Psychiatry. Lancet Psychiatry, 2017, 4:775-818

Sachdev P, Monhan A. An International Curriculum for Neuropsychiatry and Behavioural Neurology. Review of Columbia Psiquiatr, 2017, 46 (Suppl. 1):18-27

Schildkrout B et al. Integrating Neuroscience Knowledge and Neuropsychiatric Skills into Psychiatry, The Way Forward. Academic Medicine, 2016, 9:650-656

Reilly TJ. The Neurology – Psychiatry Divide: A Thought Experiment. British Journal of Psychiatry Bulletin, 2015, 39:134-135

Tracey TJ et al. Expertise in Psychotherapy: An Elusive Goal? American Psychologist, 2014, 69:218

Nawka Alexander et al. Trainees views on the Future of Psychiatry: A Plethora of Challenges. World Psychiatry, 2012, 11:203

Martin Knapp, David McDaid, Michael Parsonage (editors) Mental Health Promotion and Mental Illness prevention – The Economic Case. Department of Health, London, UK, April 2011

R.D. Laing. The Divided Self- An Existential Study of Sanity and Madness. Penguin UK, 2010

Van Praag HH. Biological Psychiatry: Still Marching Forward in a Dead End. World Psychiatry, 2010, 9:164-165

Katschnig H. Are Psychiatrists an Endangered Species? Observations on Internal and External Challenges to the Profession. World Psychiatry, 2010, 9:21-28

Awad AG, Voruganti LNP. Family Burden of Care in Schizophrenia – A Review. Pharmacoeconomics, 2008, 26:149-162

Cunningham MG et al. Coalescence of Psychiatry, Neurology and Neuropsychology – From Theory to Practice. Harvard Review of Psychiatry, 2006, 14:127-140

Gelman Sheldon. Medicating Schizophrenia – A History. Rutgers University Press, 1999

Maddox John. What Remains to be Discovered – Mapping the Secrets of the Universe, the Origins of Life and the Future of the Human Race. Free Press, 1998

Horgan John. The End of Science – Facing the Limits of Knowledge in the Twilight of the Scientific Age. Broadway Books, New York, 1996

William T. Carpenter. Psychopathology and Common Sense – Where We Went Wrong with Negative Symptoms (editorial). Biological Psychiatry, 1991, 29:735-737

Thomas Szasz. The Myth of Mental Illness. Harper & Row, 1961

BOOKS PUBLISHED BY THE AUTHOR

Evaluation of Quality of Care in Psychiatry. Pergamon Press, 1980

Disturbed Behaviour in the Elderly. Pergamon Press, 1987

Prediction of Outcome to Neuroleptic Therapy in Schizophrenia –
Conceptual and Methodological Issues. Springer Verlag, Vienna,
1994

Quality of Life Impairment in Schizophrenia, Mood and Anxiety
Disorders. Springer, 2007

Beyond Assessment of Quality of Life in Schizophrenia – Adis/
Springer, 2016

ABOUT THE AUTHOR

Photograph of the author, Dr. A.G. Awad

Dr. Awad is a Professor Emeritus in the Department of Psychiatry and on the faculty of the School of Graduate Studies at the Institute of Medical Science, University of Toronto, Canada. Dr. Awad graduated from the Faculty of Medicine, Cairo University, and completed his post-graduate studies in Cairo, Moscow, Rome and Toronto. He served in several clinical, administrative and academic roles that included serving as the Professor of Psychiatric Research, as well as the Psychiatrist-in-Chief at the Wellesley/St. Michael's Hospitals, and more recently at Humber River Hospital, in Toronto. He also served in several national and international organizations, including being elected as the first Founding President of the International Society of Central Nervous System Clinical Trials and Methodology (ISCTM). He also served as the eleventh President of the Canadian College of Neuropsychopharmacology (CCNP) and as Treasurer of the International College of Geriatric Psychopharmacology (ICGP). He served and chaired several committees in other organizations, that included the International Collegium of Neuropsychopharmacology (CINP), National Institute of Health (NIH), National Institute of Mental Health (NIMH) and the National Institute of Aging.

Dr. Awad made extensive contributions to the Canadian Psychiatric Research Foundation (CCNP), serving as a board member and Chair of the Professional Committee. He served for a few years as the editor of the Canadian Psychiatric Association's Bulletin.

For his contributions, Dr. Awad was honoured to receive several awards, including the Tanenbaum Family Award for Distinguished Scientist in Schizophrenia Research. He was awarded the CCNP medal for meritorious contributions in psychopharmacology research, teaching and services. More recently, he has received the Andrew C. Leon Distinguished Career Award in Neurosciences.

Dr. Awad is recognized for his extensive research contributions that focused on the person behind the illness. He advocated for patient-centred care, broadening concepts such as quality of life, wellness and well-being. He concluded a thirty-year study about why several patients disliked and hated to take their antipsychotic medications, by uncovering for the first time its origins in the dopamine functioning in the striatal region of the brain. In addition, Dr. Awad maintained significant clinical and research interests focused on systems and quality of psychiatric care and burden of family care. He contributed several book chapters and published several books, including his most recent book "Beyond Assessment of Quality of Life in Schizophrenia", published by Adis/Springer.

Dr. Awad is proud to have trained several generations of psychiatrists and graduate students. He continues as a national and international consultant for academic and clinical services.
Author's contact:
dr.a.g.awad2@gmail.com

Printed in the United States
by Baker & Taylor Publisher Services